7|9

FULFILLING HEART AND SOUL

Meeting Psychological and Spiritual Needs with Conscience

N. S. XAVIER, M.D.

Bloomington, IN  Milton Keynes, UK

authorHOUSE®

AuthorHouse™
1663 Liberty Drive, Suite 200
Bloomington, IN 47403
www.authorhouse.com
Phone: 1-800-839-8640

AuthorHouse™ UK Ltd.
500 Avebury Boulevard
Central Milton Keynes, MK9 2BE
www.authorhouse.co.uk
Phone: 08001974150

First published by AuthorHouse 11/9/2006

ISBN: 1-4259-7022-2 (sc)
ISBN: 1-4259-7021-4 (dj)

Library of Congress Control Number: 2006909324

Printed in the United States of America
Bloomington, Indiana

This book is printed on acid-free paper.

Although the author has made tremendous efforts to ensure the accuracy of the information contained in this book, the author and publisher assume no responsibility for errors, inaccuracies, omissions or inconsistancies. Any slights of individuals or groups are unintentional. Readers should use their own judgment and or consult appropriate experts for dealing with their individual problems. The author has used many examples from his clinical and personal experiences to illustrate his points. But he has significantly altered the identity of private persons to protect their privacy and confidentiality. Some examples are composites of similar cases.

CONTENTS

Acknowledgements of Assistance   VII

Introduction   IX

1. Make A Wonderful Transformation   1

2. Use Your Conscience Well   14

3. Stop Self-Defeating Games   33

4. Get A Perspective on Needs   46

5. Elevate Your Esteem   61

6. Keep A Healthy Identity   78

7. Relate Well   94

8. Be Powerful and Free   110

9. Integrate Your Past   124

10. Have A Balanced Present and Future   138

11. Enjoy Comfort and Pleasure   150

12. Satisfy Sexuality   162

13. Live Meaningfully   179

Conclusion   197

Appendix   205

Endnotes   209

Bibliography   213

ACKNOWLEDGEMENTS OF ASSISTANCE

I am deeply indebted to a large number of people who have generously helped me in producing this book. Regrettably, for practical reasons, the following is only a partial list.

I have relied heavily on Prof. Charles Workman (English Dept., Samford University) and my son Thomas Xavier. Prof. Fisher Humphreys has helped frequently. Prof. Jesse Milby and Prof. A.A. Khatri went over several drafts.

Prof. Wayne Oates and Dr. Gerald May, two pioneers in the mental health and spirituality field who have passed away, were highly appreciative and encouraging of this work.

Others who have provided very valuable help include the following: Prof. K.L.S. Rao, James Redfield, Dr. Godehard Oepen, Rev. Jerry Bartholow, Dr. Victor Kramer, Fr. Raymond Dunmyer, Dr. Clarence McDanal, Rev. Robert Durham, Dr. Thomas Brecht, Fr. Frank Muscolino, Fr. Greg Bittner, Rev. Ira Blanchard, Drs. A.K.B and Donna Pillai, Prof. Jane Christian, late Prof. Natwarlal Bosmia, my wife Dr. Anne Xavier, my daughter Dr. Anjali Mehra, Dr. Faye Walter, Esther Vegesina, Joe and Trish Foster, Laura Luckie, and Bobby Montano. I received editorial assistance from Loretta Cobb and Nabella Shunnarah. And several staff members at Authorhouse have been quite helpful.

INTRODUCTION

"Everything that the human race has done and thought is concerned with the satisfaction of deeply felt needs and the assuagement of pain."[1]

Albert Einstein

"The chief causes of neurosis are conflicts of conscience and difficult moral problems that require an answer."[2]

Carl Gustav Jung

If we view life closely, we can see that much human suffering and lack of psychological and spiritual fulfillment are caused by our own bad choices as individuals and groups.

We can do far better.

As a psychiatrist who has explored spirituality in depth and has used knowledge from both areas successfully in clinical practice for twenty-six years, I conclude that psychological and spiritual fulfillment depends on our pursuing good choices with the guidance of conscience and a broad understanding of human needs. This book aims to help people achieve such fulfillment.

Conflicts ranging from inner-personal and interpersonal to international can be handled constructively by using conscience properly with a good perspective on human needs.

Giving great importance to conscience, St. Paul observed that some people shipwreck their faith by rejecting conscience.[3] This is easily noticeable among people with extreme religious ideologies. When religions foster compassion, love, and wisdom, they directly or indirectly promote conscience. On the other hand, we can also find many individuals and groups using religious dogmas or ideologies to justify unreasonable and unfair deeds. In such cases, "conscience is anesthetized by dogmas,"[4] as Hindu philosopher Sarvepalli Radhakrishnan has noted. By promoting conscience, religion and culture can nurture psychological and spiritual fulfillment and prevent much suffering.

In dealing with our various needs, conscience, if properly used, can guide us quite well. Conscience promotes faith without fanaticism, individuality without selfishness, discipline without rigidity, pleasure without addiction, self-esteem without false pride, loyalty to one's group without unfairness to other groups, integration of the past without impediment to the present, future direction without loss of balance, good judgment without prejudices, and deep morality without superficial moralism. A society of people guided by conscience would manifest law and order without legalism and militarism. Such a society would encourage interdependence and genuine individuality with a spirit of fairness and responsibility toward oneself, fellow humans, and the world.

In guiding our choices, conscience uses reason regarding what is good for ourselves in the long run and is fair to others by the Golden Rule--to do to others as we would have them do to us. The spirit of the Golden Rule   includes respecting other people's differences. George Bernard Shaw had suggested that we must not do to others as we would have them do to us because their tastes may differ from ours. Our tastes are related to our needs. While awake, we are constantly faced with choices relevant to human needs. And it is in making these choices that we use, evade or contradict our consciences. A good perspective on human needs is, therefore, crucial in using our consciences properly.

People are often confused about conscience because we have another inner judge that I call the "superego." The superego judges what is good or bad by what one has picked up and internalized as good or bad from family and society. Superego's judgment may or may not be in harmony with conscience. Judgments of superegos shaped by wrong influences from family or society are likely to be unreasonable and unfair. For instance, children who are unreasonably criticized about their choices are likely to develop harsh superegos and judge themselves unfairly regarding their choices.

People often mistake the superego for the conscience and may not really use the conscience. A great deal of conflict and suffering is caused by individuals following their superegos with unreasonable and unfair standards in handling their needs.

We have psychological and spiritual needs. Our psychological needs involve our physical, social, and emotional well-being. These include needs for esteem and value system, identity, relationships, power, integration of the past, present balance and future direction, pleasure, sexual satisfaction, and meaning. Our spiritual needs add a deeper dimension to all these psychological needs. For example, spiritual meaning goes beyond social meaning and includes belief in God or a spiritual realm. While each need can be met in different ways, meeting various needs with conscience is the most balanced, efficient, and integrated way to lead a psychologically and spiritually fulfilling life.

Priority of needs differs among individuals. While one person's priority may be power, another's priority may be pleasure. Intensity of needs also varies. Sexual needs may vary from more than once a day to not even once a month. People handle different needs in different ways including immediate or delayed gratification, and partial or total denial. Such differences regarding human needs cause much confusion and conflict among people. Moreover, people may persist in their patterns of dealing with needs without reflecting on them and making useful changes. In such a case, one man continued to reject his fiancé's show of affection by saying, "Don't pat me; I am not a dog." Finally, she rejected him.

Often, however, neither conscience nor superego may be utilized to guide choices when a person is driven by an intense need. Excessive attachment to one need at the expense of other needs tends to cause emotional and spiritual distress. People can become "basket cases" by putting too many eggs into one basket. This is reminiscent of how wild monkeys are caught by some people by making an opening in a coconut just big enough to let a monkey's hand go in, putting peanuts inside, and attaching the coconut to a tree where monkeys are found. The monkey that puts one hand in and holds on to the peanuts gets caught because it cannot free the hand. Like freedom for such monkeys, the possibility of healthy transformation for humans involves relinquishing excessive focus on one need and finding overall fulfillment.

A good example of such transformation is Kathy, an accountant in her thirties, who was abused in her childhood. When she saw me, she already had many years of psychotherapy and several hospitalizations and was on several medications. She had become intensely fixated on her past. For over a year her work and her social, spiritual, intellectual, and artistic interests had been mostly on hold. She had good intentions in trying to heal her old wounds. But her excessive focus on those wounds resulted in even stronger ties to her past, more imbalances in her present life, and worse problems for her future. Thus, she had become sicker. I helped her to make two changes: have a good perspective on her overall needs and use her conscience to guide her choices in meeting those needs. To use her conscience, I taught her to distinguish between the judgments of her conscience and the distorted judgments of her harsh superego shaped by her abusive family. She used to judge herself harshly by her superego and feel guilt and shame unreasonably even when she made the right choices within her limits. As she pursued these changes, in a few months she began living a fulfilling life.

A secret to helping others transform is to understand their needs and show them better alternatives to meet those needs. This method is dramatically illustrated in Steven Spielberg's acclaimed film *Schindler's List*. The movie's hero Oskar Schindler observes a Nazi officer killing Jewish prisoners in a concentration camp. One day when the officer is drinking, Schindler questions him and realizes that the man is killing his victims because of his need for power. Then Schindler convinces the officer to stop killing by explaining to him that he can have more power by pardoning. Schindler succeeded because he understood the need behind the officer's evil actions and provided a better alternative to deal with the need.

An ethical sense of what is good or bad is essential in   fulfilling our overall needs, especially our spiritual needs. If we satisfy our psychological needs by wrong means which contradict our consciences, we damage our spiritual wellness. In numerous cases, I have helped people to find fulfillment by clearing their confusion about conscience and showing them how to use this wonderful spiritual guide in making good choices to deal with their needs.

An old saying, "When the mystic points to the moon the idiots see only the finger," indicates our tendency to focus on the superficial and miss the broader perspective. We can make our lives far more fulfilling by meeting our deeper needs than by spending our resources on superficial pursuits. Similarly, in the coming chapters we will dig deeper and find great treasures of wisdom in many interesting sacred as well as secular stories. Such wisdom can empower us to be our best individually and collectively.

Although the eminent psychiatrist Carl Jung emphasized the importance of conscience, the mental health field has largely neglected or misunderstood conscience. The biggest challenge, best opportunity, and greatest common ground for the mental health and religious/ spiritual fields are to promote psychological and spiritual fulfillment by helping people use conscience and good insight into human needs. Unlike promoting a particular religious group's ideology, which can cause ethical conflict for mental health professionals, I do not see such conflict in providing people a perspective on conscience and superego as well as human needs.

In a world where people of various cultures and religions interact closely, there is great benefit in using the guidance of conscience rather than fostering misguided faiths or destructive attitudes and deeds by rejecting conscience. Those who don't want to use their consciences or consider their superegos as their consciences can at least recognize that there is a different perspective. Those who don't believe in a spiritual level can still benefit from insights into human needs and conscience, as these insights can help greatly in leading deeply ethical lives.

1. MAKE A WONDERFUL TRANSFORMATION

"It is wonderful and hard to believe how my husband has changed--from being selfish, angry, and very depressed to being loving and happy."

--wife of a patient

"**Y**ou have really turned my life around. I have been using what I learned from you. I feel great emotionally and spiritually," reported Alice, a beautiful blonde teacher in her thirties, on a follow up visit after hospitalization for depression with suicidal thoughts. Her story is a good example of wonderful transformation.

Alice was a hard working, intelligent, and caring person but she never felt she was good enough for her judgmental mother. Alice's husband, Allen, was preoccupied for a few months with his new job and some problems caused by his ex-wife. He had paid Alice less attention during those months, and they had argued more. Alice had a difficult boss. She had been excessively self-critical from her childhood, and this tendency became worse with more stress. She used alcohol at times to relieve her stress, and her drinking had begun to get out of control. Hating herself for all of these faults and failures, she seriously considered suicide. At this point, she realized she needed intensive professional help, and she was hospitalized.

Alice's face turned red and her eyes became moist as she recalled how hurt she was in her childhood because of her mother's criticism and control and her father's emotional distance. Her usually low self-esteem plummeted prior to her hospitalization as she judged herself worthless.

The more she focused on her real and imagined faults, the worse her self-hate became. I tried first to help her replace her harmful judgment of herself with a judgment that would promote healing and fulfillment.

I told Alice that often I utilize a Biblical story very successfully to explain to people--no matter what their religious beliefs--the two kinds of judgments we use. She was eager for me to proceed. Alice had read the Bible, but she had forgotten much of the story of a woman who was caught in the act of adultery. So I told her the story as recounted in the Gospel of John 8:2-11.

A group of men brought the adulterous woman before Jesus to tempt Him into making a wrong judgment so that they could use that decision against Him. They reminded Him that, according to the Law of Moses, she should be stoned to death. Silent at first, Jesus stooped and wrote something on the ground. Then He stood up and said, "He that is without sin among you, let him first cast a stone at her." Then He stooped again and wrote on the ground. The men left one by one "convicted by their own conscience," and Jesus told the woman that He did not condemn her but she should stop her sinful behavior.

With a reflective look, Alice said: "Please tell me what I can learn from it."

I answered: "Just imagine the emotional intensity of those men who were dealing with three big issues: being with a woman freshly caught committing adultery, thinking of stoning her to death according to religious law, and testing a new spiritual teacher. Driven by such sexual, aggressive, and religious passions, what would they have done if Jesus were also highly emotional and had argued with them?"

"The guys would have gotten madder and acted violently," Alice replied.

I concurred and went on: "Jesus prevented the escalation of tension by avoiding a heated argument. He calmed them by being calm and using a calming distraction (like a hypnotist using a swinging watch) by writing on the ground. Then Jesus challenged them with the spirit of the Golden Rule. If we are too emotional, it is hard for us to use our consciences."

"Why did Jesus say, 'he among you who has not sinned throw the first stone' instead of 'those of you who have not sinned throw stones'?" I asked.

Alice reflected for a few minutes and answered: "Then they might have thrown stones. Often, in a group, people might focus on impressing others more than on reflecting deeply within their own hearts to decide what is right."

Agreeing with Alice, I posed another question: "Why did Jesus say 'he who has not sinned' rather than 'he who has not committed adultery'?"

Alice replied quickly: "Because some of them may not have committed adultery but have sinned in other ways."

Again I agreed, adding: "We have to expand our imagination and utilize our empathy, compassion or love to apply the spirit of the Golden Rule. In judging what is good, conscience uses the Golden Rule of fairness and justice to others and the ethical principle of doing what is good--or useful and not harmful--for oneself in the long run. So conscience is driven by reason and love or compassion for oneself and others. If we want to utilize conscience properly we have to use calm reflection and reasoning, keeping our minds open to information from various sources instead of just one view we may have learned from our family or society. Jesus stimulated the men's consciences but when they came to Jesus they were using their socially programmed judgment of right and wrong, what I call their superegos."

Alice was tearful as she reflected briefly. Then she said calmly: "Now I see my biggest problem. I have been judging myself by my superego which was mostly shaped by my mother. So I have been throwing stones at myself. I have also been too judgmental of Allen since we became intimate. In fact, the other day when I let him really have it, he told me I sounded just like my mother. It infuriated me because I didn't want to admit the unpleasant truth." Wiping her tears, she said: "So, you are telling me that I should use my conscience and judge with reason, compassion, and love. I will work on it."

Alice worked on using the guidance of her conscience. She joked about how her overgrown superego was shrinking because she was not using it much, and how the term "shrink" used for psychiatrists truly applied to me in her case. Her superego would not give up easily; it tried numerous times to sneak up and attack her with destructive criticisms, but Alice gradually got stronger in recognizing and letting go of those harmful judgments from her "inner enemy" ("inner terrorist," "inside dictator," "my demon," "the committee" are other terms some patients have used).

My next effort was to help her meet her overall needs consistent with her conscience. We explored her needs in terms of the list of human needs on pages 46-47, and many changes she could make to lead a fulfilling life.

As we explored these, Alice realized that she was driven by strong unfulfilled needs for esteem, power, and close harmonious relationships. She felt these needs too strongly for several reasons: 1) These needs were not satisfied at all in her childhood. She was like a person who was too hungry at dinner time because she had missed breakfast and lunch. 2) Her harsh superego abused her and kept her self-esteem low even when she was doing her best. 3) She felt powerless with her superego and her mother. She tried extra hard to gain a sense of power from work. 4) She needed strong support from others to neutralize the attacks from her own inner enemy. Also, even useful criticisms from others were too painful for her because of her own excessive self-criticism. Conflicts with others made her insecurity and low self-esteem worse, causing her to be a "people pleaser" who avoided facing conflicts with others.

She had neglected her other needs including meaning and pleasure. She gradually realized that these imbalances in her attempts to meet her needs resulted in the lack of fulfillment in her life. Often she had feelings of guilt, shame, insecurity, frustration, emptiness, and anger. With therapy Alice learned the connection between these feelings and her needs, and how she could use her conscience to guide her in dealing with these needs. She learned to tune down excessive feelings using her understanding of them, utilizing relaxation techniques, and focusing on useful action instead of harmful feelings. She began to meet her needs for meaning and pleasure as well as other needs. She quit drinking and used healthy relaxation techniques.

As she developed a deeper understanding of herself she recognized the needs behind the actions of others too. So she dealt with them effectively and faced conflicts realistically. She met her various needs in a balanced pattern. Her self-hate was replaced by healthy love of self, which made her relationship to others more loving too. Through her struggles to transform, she gained a great deal of wisdom. These changes made her life fulfilling.

A GREAT CLASSICAL STORY OF TRANSFORMATION

French novelist Victor Hugo, who was so popular that two million people reportedly turned out for his funeral in 1885, provides a marvelous story of transformation of the criminal Jean Valjean, in the classic *Les Miserables*. Although I have found many people who knew the story, they had not fully grasped many of the profound insights in this novel. Interestingly, Jean's change from a convict to a good man was based on a real-life incident between a criminal and a bishop. Jean, who lost his parents in childhood, was reared by his sister. After his sister's husband died, Jean worked to support the family. One winter he had no work, and the family had no bread. Jean stole a loaf of bread for which he was sentenced to five years in prison, but he spent nineteen years there because he made five futile attempts to escape.

Jean knew that he did wrong in stealing the bread and that he could have probably gotten it by asking the shopkeeper. But by the time he came out of prison, he hated society and had become a dangerous man who never smiled and rarely spoke. No one would give him a meal even though he was willing to pay for it.

At someone's suggestion, Jean knocked at the door of a bishop. The elderly bishop was a man of conscience, a good and compassionate person who lived a simple and happy life. The bishop treated Jean with respect, shared his supper with him, and offered him a place to sleep.

Jean had noticed the bishop's silver plates and silver candlesticks. That night Jean stole the silver plates and left. The police caught him and brought him to the bishop who pretended that he had given Jean the plates and even gave him the candlesticks. So the police freed him. The bishop urged Jean to use the silver to become an honest man, adding: "Jean Valjean, my brother, you belong no longer to evil but to good."[5]

Jean had known only hard work, poverty, and the harshness of prison life. The bishop's compassion, goodness, and appeal to Jean's conscience stimulated his conscience but it did not change him immediately. As he walked around, he stole a coin accidentally dropped by a poor boy who ran away crying. Soon a change came over Jean, and he tried in vain to find the boy and return the coin. Then, with a conscience burdened with guilt, he cried for the first time in nineteen years. Such guilt about one's wrongdoing is a powerful force for transformation.

Jean's conscience had been stimulated to change, but his personality resisted that change. He used pride--"the fortress of evil in man"[6]--in his resistance. But the strong impact of the Bishop made Jean, using his conscience, review the evils of his past. His conscience finally won. Afterward Jean remained a man of compassion, love, and wisdom through many trials and triumphs of his life.

Hugo says of the bishop's conscience: "The souls of the upright in sleep contemplate a mysterious heaven... this heaven was within him; it was his conscience."[7] Had the bishop simply allowed himself to be robbed, it could have reinforced Jean's criminality. As Behavioral Psychology teaches, rewards increase and punishments decrease a behavior, but conscience works beyond this level. For instance, a person guided by conscience would take punishment and do what he/she judges as the good or right choice. Jean's slumbering conscience was awakened by the impact of the bishop's penetrating words coupled with his acts of compassion and love. Words alone would have fallen on deaf ears. Human beings have the potential to function at the behavioral level as well as at the level of conscience. Many people fail to recognize the benefits of stimulating conscience because their views are fixated at the behavioral level.

Subsequently, Jean encountered many opportunities to use his compassion and love, especially in bringing up a beautiful little girl, Cosette, whose mother had died of illness in spite of Jean's attempts to help her. Hugo also depicts a merciless and authoritarian police officer named Javert, who was clearly driven by a harsh superego. Javert's superego was shaped by having been born in prison and growing up with an exaggerated respect for authority, hatred of his own gypsy race, and disgust for those who ever broke a law. He knew that Jean had stolen from the Bishop and the poor boy. Javert pursued Jean and again put him in prison, but Jean escaped. Jean continued to take care of Cosette and do many other good deeds.

Later, Jean saved Javert's life from a group of rebels. The next time they crossed paths, Javert did not incarcerate Jean. The kindness of the convict Jean astonished Javert and he was petrified by his own kind response. Javert judged his action by his harsh superego and found it an appalling infraction. It created unbearable inner turmoil and he committed suicide. Had he used his conscience, he would have felt inner peace and he could have made a far better choice than suicide. One of his choices would have been to reveal to his authorities what he had done and take the consequence, as people do in civil disobedience.

Among the hundreds of suicide attempts I have dealt with, a great percentage have been prompted by the individuals' superegos, but none from their consciences. Human resistance to change, the power of conscience to transform, and the damages caused by distorted superegos are common experiences in my work.

A Clinical Case of Awakening of Conscience

I used the technique of stimulating conscience with Doug. He had quit school and was abusing alcohol and drugs and manipulating his parents to get money. Although Doug had treatments at some nationally famous psychiatric facilities previously, he had shown no lasting progress. He had rejected his parents' religious beliefs because they did not fit his intellectual outlook. Doug had an air of superiority based on his intelligence, but his self-esteem was low because he lacked achievements.

I developed a rapport with Doug, but he was irregular in attending therapy, and prone to lying and manipulating. He shared some of his secrets with me, but he did not make significant progress until he had a crisis from a broken relationship. He was hospitalized with depression.

Doug was now willing to cooperate, but based on his past I knew that he would revert to his old ways unless I could make a strong impact while he was hospitalized. I asked him to make a list of all the very harmful and unfair things he had done and how badly these things had hurt himself and others. My purpose was to stimulate Doug's conscience, which he had neglected for years, so he would experience as much realistic guilt as possible. Then I would help him repair the damage he had caused as well as avoid repeating the destructive behaviors.

Doug spent a sleepless and tearful night writing down his list. The next day we reviewed what he had written and discussed how he deserved to feel guilt for the wrongs he had done. I explained to him the function of conscience and how he could use his guilt to transform his life. For the next several days, we went over his wrongs, his repentance and how he could repair many of the damages he had caused and prevent repeating the wrongs in the future. Doug said he had never felt so remorseful.

He expressed his remorse to his parents and asked for their forgiveness, which set the stage for a healthy relationship with them. He cut off his drug connections and started benefiting from Narcotics Anonymous meetings. Doug had not benefited from self-help groups previously because of his sick pride--he used to merely argue against the therapeutic steps or against the group. While he was feeling guilty and his arrogance was low, I pointed out how he was using his intelligence to evade rather than utilize his conscience, and he worked to change that pattern.

We also discussed how he could meet his various needs in healthy ways. After leaving the hospital he started working, stayed drug free, related well to his family, and had a healthy spirituality guided by his conscience.

Living by our consciences involves controlling our impulses and temptations as the next example illustrates.

Controlling the PIG--Problem of Irrational Gratification

As I was shopping one day, I heard a voice saying: "Hi doc!" It was Linda, a former patient, beaming with a big smile. She used to have problems with depression, overeating, drug addiction, and conflicts in her relationships because of her temper. Her loose superego accepted her impulsive choices and she hardly used her conscience in those years. So she had no guilt, but she had a lot of frustration and anger when things did not go her way. She used to make choices often by her intense desire for immediate gratification. She had a severe problem of irrational gratification (PIG).

Linda said: "You will be proud of me. I have kept my PIG in good control. Remember you used to tell me that if I let my PIG be in the driver's seat, it would drive me up the wall and down into the ditch. After being off the wall and in the ditch many times, tamed the pig before it turned into a wild boar or pieces of bacon. I use my conscience, exercise, meditate, pray, and eat right. When I think of doing harmful things, my conscience rings the alarm and I back off and feel good about controlling the pig. I have held a good job for a couple of years. I control my temper and get along well with my boyfriend and my father. You know how he used to fuss, and I used to get mad. Thanks to you I am happy. I *meet my needs in tune with my conscience* as you told me."

I was delighted to hear such a progress report. "Keep up the wonderful changes," I said as we parted.

Therapeutic dose of guilt/shame

The above cases teach us a vital lesson. Like taking the right dose of medicine, we benefit greatly from enough guilt or shame to prevent or correct wrongdoing. An overdose or an inadequate dose of these feelings can harm us. Conscience, when properly used, stimulates a therapeutic dose of guilt or shame, motivating us to regenerate from degenerated states. A harsh superego tends to cause excessive guilt or shame and a loose superego tends to cause very little or no guilt or shame.

THE REGENERATIVE POWER OF CONSCIENCE

The power of conscience can regenerate both individuals and communities. Mahatma Gandhi, who was chosen by *Time* magazine as one of the two runners-up for "Person of the Century," changed the course of history by using his own conscience and helping his followers as well as his foes to transform by stimulating their consciences. By nonviolent mass movement Gandhi was able to change the attitude of the British colonialists and eventually gain freedom for India. Gandhi also significantly reformed the age-old caste system of Hindu society, which was very unfair to the "untouchables," the lowest group in that system. Gandhi's nonviolent approaches were adopted by Martin Luther King, Jr. in the civil rights movement. These movements used the power of conscience against unfair systems often supported by people with unreasonable superegos.

Gandhi himself was influenced by Leo Tolstoy's insights on conscience. In *The Kingdom of God Is Within You*, one of the few books that most influenced Gandhi, Tolstoy notes the role of conscience: "our life... can have no significance except in the constant accomplishment of what is demanded by the Power which has placed us in life with a sole certain guide--the rational conscience."[8]

In Tolstoy's short story *The Chinese Pilot*, many people belonging to different religions and nations argue about God and the proper way to worship him. Finally, the best informed person in the group, the Chinese Pilot, posed several questions, including "Where is there any book of law so clear as that written in his heart? What sacrifices equal the self-denials which loving men and women make for one another? And what altar can be compared with the heart of a good man, on which God himself accepts the sacrifice?"[9] These are worthy questions to ponder regarding conscience.

Tolstoy divided people into freethinkers and others. "Freethinkers are those who are willing to use their minds without prejudice and without fearing to understand things that clash with their own customs, privileges or beliefs."[10] Such openness of mind is essential for using conscience quite well.

A touching scene in the movie *Gandhi* shows a poor Hindu, full of rage and fear, telling Gandhi that he is going to hell for killing a Muslim boy in revenge for Muslims killing his son. Gandhi empathizes with the man and tells him that he can avoid hell by bringing up an orphan Muslim boy in Islam. The man pays his respects to Gandhi and leaves in peace. By appealing to the man's conscience, Gandhi motivated his reparation and regeneration.

TRANSFORMATION OF CHARACTER AND JUDGING CHARACTER

Character or second nature is a person's pattern of thinking and behaving. All the above examples of change involved transformation of character from unhealthy to healthy ones. Such transformations are far more difficult to produce and maintain than temporary changes in behavior under external pressure or for short-term gain. This is one reason for skepticism about someone who claims to have changed.

As conscience evaluates our choices and actions, it notices our pattern of behavior and approves or disapproves of our character. Thus, people living by conscience will have good self-esteem if they also judge themselves fairly. I have had many patients who lived by their consciences but judged their worthiness unfairly by their harsh superegos and therefore had poor self-esteem. As I taught them to judge their character also by their consciences, they began to feel good about themselves. I recall the joyful excitement of a patient as I taught her this--her face lit up as she exclaimed: "Oh! A light just went on in my head!" She was a good person who looked down on herself for not being too successful by the standards of society. That insight was a turning point in her life.

Transforming Relationships

Ted and Tipper were both depressed, and their marriage was in serious trouble when they started seeing me. Both were caught up in their own needs in self-defeating ways rather than understanding and helping each other to fulfill their needs. Ted grew up in an insecure home with a verbally abusive father who unreasonably doubted the faithfulness of his wife. The father did not work regularly, causing the family financial hardship. Consequently, financial security, relationship issues, and the need to vent his negative feelings became significant for Ted. Therefore, he overworked without much time for fun, dominated his wife, and, like his father, nagged her about her fidelity.

Tipper had strict parents who were financially poor, not very affectionate, and excessively controlling and judgmental. So she liked the financial security and relationship commitment Ted provided, but disliked his control and criticism. He did not meet her strong need for affection and sense of attractiveness. Although their biological sex drives were similar, they had intense sexual conflicts. Ted needed excessive assurance of Tipper's fidelity and often expressed his doubts to receive reassurance. Such behavior, along with his not meeting her needs for affection and sense of attractiveness turned her off. He didn't believe in complimenting her about her attractiveness for fear of giving her a "big head". Ted became more suspicious as he noticed Tipper's dampened interest in sex, thinking she might be having an affair.

In dealing with them I told the story of a rabbi who visited hell and heaven. In both places the people had beautiful dining rooms with plenty of wonderful food, but they had to eat without bending their elbows. In hell the people were starving and miserable, and the dining rooms were filthy with food which spilt over as they tried to eat without bending their elbows. In heaven, however, people were well-fed and happy and the dining rooms were clean because they were feeding each other without bending their elbows. In hell the people not only did not care about others, but they also did not take a broad look at their situation, reevaluate their actions and learn from their failures. They remained "hell bent" on being rigidly consistent and proud of it, as such people are.

Using this story, I discussed how they could understand and help each other meet their needs and enjoy fulfilling lives. I explained to them the various human needs, and how individuals differ in what particular need is more important to them, and how people take different approaches to meet their needs. We also discussed how they could use their consciences to guide their choices in meeting their needs and feel good about doing so. Thus, they could enhance their self-esteem by making reasonable changes to accommodate the spouse's needs, rather than consider themselves "losers" for giving up some old ways. With these changes, they related well and enjoyed fulfilling lives.

People are far more willing to accept and try to accommodate someone's pattern of behavior if the pattern is seen as reasonable based on a genuine human need. Knowing human needs in general helps tremendously to understand the real needs behind our own and others' wants, feelings, actions, and reactions. Such understanding is crucial in effectively using our consciences to make fulfilling choices and in helping others to do so. We also have to be cautious to prevent being misled by the pressure of certain needs or by wrong judgments from our superegos. Thus, a good perspective on one's needs and being guided well by one's conscience go hand in hand in leading a psychologically and spiritually fulfilling life.

There is much more to understanding and utilizing conscience and superego which we will get into next.

2. Use Your Conscience Well

As spiritual and social beings capable of judging what is good and bad or right and wrong, we have two inner guides, conscience and superego, as we saw in the previous chapter. We can consider conscience as the spiritual guide and superego the social guide in a person. Learning to use these two guides well is crucial to fulfill our hearts and souls or to meet our psychological and spiritual needs.

Conscience and Superego

In the biblical story of the adulterous woman we saw the men first using their superegos and then their consciences in their judgment. Superego and conscience may be used to judge before, during, and after an action.

As social beings, we develop superegos from the views, values, and examples of our parents and significant others. Just as in animals, our behavior can be conditioned by rewards and punishments. For us, acceptance by others is a reward and rejection a punishment. Superego is also shaped by our tendency to conform to the group. Peers, authorities, and the media influence the shaping of one's superego.

At a deeper--what I view as the spiritual--level, we have conscience, the capacity to judge what is good or bad using reason and the Golden Rule. Applying reason and the Golden Rule involves love and compassion in varying degrees. The love and compassion are strongest towards ourselves and those close to us and less towards others but at least a sense of fairness is present towards all including enemies. Ancient Greeks had the concept of conscience, and the term was coined by the Greeks and Romans. Socrates spoke of his conscience as his indwelling divine monitor. Great thinkers like Seneca, Cicero, and Philo of Alexandria gave tremendous importance to this inner divine guide.

The Catholic Church's Vatican II Council of bishops described it as a law inscribed in human heart by God. *"Its voice, ever calling him to love and to do what is good and to avoid evil, tells him inwardly at the right moment: do this, shun that... His dignity lies in observing this law, and by it he will be judged."*[12] According to theologian Paul Tillich, Christianity has always maintained that people have a moral obligation to obey their consciences. Tillich added that St. Paul, Catholic theologian Thomas Aquinas, and Martin Luther agreed on this point, and they kept the authority of conscience in the ethical--not religious--sphere.[13] One does not have to be religious to use one's conscience.

Conscience, motivated by love, compassion or fairness, and guided by reason with an open mind, promotes what is useful for oneself and others. Conscience supports self-discipline to pursue the useful and reject the harmful choice even if it provides immediate pleasure, power or prestige. When conscience signals fear or anxiety, it is warning us against doing something harmful or unfair. When it evokes guilt or shame, it is pushing us to recognize and correct our wrongs and avoid repeating the mistakes.

Healthy social influences such as wise teachings and good role models, promote the function of conscience in people by helping them use their own reason, empathy, compassion, and love. This is quite different from social conditioning by reward and punishment--acting like a trained animal or blindly conforming to a group or a model. Conscience promotes not simply right behavior, it promotes right behavior for the right reason with right motivation and openness of mind.

People who act according to their consciences show the courage to go against the tendency to follow the herd. For instance, many whites used their consciences and participated in the civil rights movement in spite of rejection and retaliation by their own communities. Such choices show the human capacity to use one's free will. Conscience promotes the healthy use of free will.

Conscience and Heart--The Heart of the Matter

St. Paul called conscience "the law written in the heart"(Romans 2:15). In the Old Testament God told His people He would write the law in their hearts (Jeremiah 31:33). Conscience judges with a loving/compassionate heart.

Human-heartedness ("jen" in Chinese) is the most important virtue according to Confucius. It involves a strong sense of human dignity, goodness, diligence in work, empathy, and magnanimity. In fourth century B. C., Mencius, a great follower of Confucius, taught that the heavenly gift of a thinking heart distinguishes human beings from animals. Without using this gift we are no better than animals. He attributes to the thinking heart the qualities of modesty, compassion, shame, and the sense of right and wrong.

In Hinduism, the moral code known as the *Laws of Manu* uses the satisfaction of one's heart as one of the tests to determine whether a choice is morally good. Also the epic *Mahabharata* teaches that along with the example set by good people, what is morally good is what is sanctioned by an honest heart.

Compassion, one of the central tenets of Buddhism, is the quality of the heart. Compassion and wisdom go together, and the Buddha taught not to rely on the ordinary judgmental mind but rely on the wise mind. When we judge with our wise minds in making choices we are using our consciences.

The Koran states that God inspired the soul as to what is right and wrong for it (Sura 91:8). According to Islamic mystic Jalaluddin Rumi, we find God's Light in our hearts. Compassion is emphasized by Islam.

Other religions such as Zoroastrianism, Taoism, Jainism, Sikhism, and Baha'i Faith also promote compassion. All religions teach the Golden Rule in different ways.

By focusing on the heart, I am not promoting a sentimental, "bleeding-heart" approach. I do firmly believe in the discipline and responsibility demanded by conscience. To live by conscience, we must not follow the passions of the heart lawlessly or pursue the laws heartlessly.

Interestingly, Adam Smith, who is famous for his economic theory, wrote *The Theory of Moral Sentiments* in 1759 in which he gave great importance to conscience. He referred to conscience as the impartial spectator and the great judge and arbiter of conduct. Moreover, he considered conscience a much higher tribunal than the judgment and approval or disapproval of fellow members of society.

Like many religious advocates, Christian thinker C. S. Lewis used the existence of conscience, which he called Law of Nature, as evidence of a spiritual reality. Notable among individuals strongly influenced by Lewis' view is the famous scientist Francis Collins, National Human Genome Research Director, who turned from atheism to a belief in God.

A STEP FURTHER THAN FREUD

In Freud's view, the superego, the judicial branch of one's personality, develops by assimilating the standards of one's parents regarding what is good and bad. It has two parts--the conscience which dictates what one should not do and the ego-ideal which prescribes what one should do. He referred to the following statement by Philosopher Emmanuel Kant: "Two things incline the heart to wonder, the moral law within and the starry sky above." And Freud remarked: "...as regards conscience God has done an uneven and careless piece of work, for a large majority of men have brought along with them only a modest amount of it or scarcely enough to be worth mentioning.... Even if conscience is something within us it is not so from the first."[14]

I believe the superego is conditioned by the standards of parents and society including religion. And I believe conscience is not simply a part of superego but another inner judging faculty as I have described. My concept of conscience is along the lines of the spiritual/philosophical traditions I have noted.

HOW CAN WE USE CONSCIENCE WELL?

There are four steps in using our conscience well:

Awareness or knowledge of choices and decisions we are faced with; *Decision* or choosing a course of action; *Action;* and *Reassessment* or reevaluation of the decision and action based on the results of the action.

1. *Awareness.* The words "conscience" and "consciousness" have a common root. Conscience is judging with consciousness or awareness. We become aware of the pros and cons of various choices regarding whatever it is we are considering. Openness of mind, respect for truth, and input from external and internal sources are important for strong awareness. Input from external sources includes knowledge about our needs and what are healthy and unhealthy methods of dealing with our needs. On these matters we get information, ideas, and ideals from family, society, religions, educational sources, and the media. Some such information may be correct and useful while other may be incorrect and misleading. So, we must be careful to use our intelligence and consciences properly to make correct choices. Ideas from our family and culture as well as insights from religious, ethical, and scientific (especially psychological) sources are particularly useful.

A person of conscience is open to new knowledge. In the light of better knowledge, an action we once considered right in the past may turn out to be wrong, or the other way around. For example, many people say they enjoyed smoking cigarettes as a harmless and pleasant habit many years ago. But once the harmful consequences of smoking were known, they felt guilty if they smoked. In the opposite way, a conscientious woman who caught AIDS from a blood transfusion stopped even hugging her children for fear of spreading the disease. Once she realized that the disease would not spread by hugging or kissing on their cheeks, her conscience allowed her to show affection in those ways again.

Input from ourselves involves our feelings, thoughts, and lessons from past experiences. The practice of solitude or calm reflection helps to strengthen and integrate awareness from different sources. For instance, a middle-aged woman who was depressed for many years had a rigid superego and much self-hate. When she was with her family, her superego was too active; she felt rejected and got mired in self-hate. But when she enjoyed solitude, such as when she took walks alone in the woods, she could calmly feel, think, and judge by her conscience instead of her superego.

Meditation and reflection can foster solitude, thereby enhancing the utilization of conscience. Solitude also helps in the next step of using conscience--decision.

2. *Decision*. This step involves first assessing our options, applying the principles of what is good or useful for ourselves and fair and responsible to others. We then plan the course of action. In making the right choice (and in the next step of acting on it), we need understanding--broad perspective of our own needs and deep empathic knowledge of others' needs.

Understanding our own and others' needs involves having a broad perspective on various human needs. For instance, Roger, a Christian minister who was working too hard without enough rest and recreation, felt rejected by some prominent members of his congregation when they criticized his tired appearance and diminished enthusiasm. Then his superego stimulated excessive guilt and shame, and this inner turmoil caused him to function even worse. I helped him to have a broad perspective on human needs and recognize the importance of the need for rest and recreation along with nutrition and sleep. I also helped him to judge by his conscience and not by his punitive superego which was shaped by harsh parents. Moreover, I pointed out to him that he could use feedback from others as input for his conscience, not as a weapon for his superego to abuse him. As he made these changes, he was not only happier but also a far better spiritual person and more effective leader who could help others fulfill their hearts and souls.

A broad perspective on human needs is essential for understanding others well, too. As Roger understood his own needs better and became more aware of human needs in general, his capacity for empathy increased greatly. Empathy is the imaginative ability to understand and vicariously experience another's feelings, thoughts, and actions.

Empathic capacity gives us access to other people's inner world. Then we have the power to use that access with compassion and love or with selfishness or even hate. If we are guided by our consciences, we would use our knowledge about another with compassion and love. I have found many happy marriages where the spouses have keen knowledge about the strengths and weaknesses of their partners and actively help to build on their strengths and heal their weaknesses. I have also seen many miserable marriages where the spouses know and exploit each other's weaknesses. Those who push each other's buttons or one spouse exploiting the weakness of the other may enjoy some sense of power but the overall effect is lack of psychological and spiritual fulfillment. Such people are not guided by their consciences and they lack a good perspective on human needs. The better we understand humanity, the more compassion and love we have.

Compassion and love overlap and reinforce each other. Compassion involves understanding of suffering and the motivation to relieve it. The keener our perception of human needs, the more compassion we have about the suffering caused by unfulfilled needs. Love involves nurturing to fulfill the needs of ourselves and others. Here again, the keener our understanding of human needs and the better we meet those needs, the stronger our love. In compassion the emphasis is on relieving suffering, and in love the emphasis is on nurturing. When we are doubtful about a choice, we can try to find the correct answer by getting more information and seeking advice from others, especially experts on the matter. If still unsure of the right choice, we can choose the safer course of action.

3. *Action.* We act based on the decision we have made.

Discipline is very important in carrying out our decisions. Based on past distortions, many people mistake discipline for rigidity. *My definition of discipline is beautiful behavior.* And what is beautiful, like paintings and music, has harmonious, neither rigid nor loose, limits.

Moderation is the key to healthy discipline. Military discipline is appropriate only in a military situation. A military man who enforced rigid discipline at home for several years realized in therapy that he had to loosen up at home or lose his family. As he went beyond his superficial and rigid ideals of right and wrong, he developed a broader, more useful perspective on life. Consequently, he could, without getting angry, ignore his teenagers wearing their caps backwards or using slang, and focus on engaging them in conversations about deeper matters such as studies, dating, and spirituality.

I had explained to him the difference between superego and conscience and how his rigid superego narrowed his perspective and caused his discipline to be extreme. As he used the guidance of his conscience and exercised moderation along with deeper understanding and broader perspective, he gained inner peace and a happy relationship with his family.

Discipline is not simply a matter of just saying "no" to certain desires connected with our needs. Rather, discipline involves four elements: Caution, Courage, Nurturing, and Insight combined with wisdom.

a.) *Caution* or delaying gratification--controlling the PIG or the problem of irrational gratification as we noted in Chapter One--is a big part of discipline. A pig not only eats but also relieves its discomforts indiscriminately without delay. Likewise, many people have difficulty in delaying their need for comfort and pleasure, and for relieving their discomfort and pain. Although conscience prompts us to delay or deny impulses and desires that are harmful to ourselves or others, conscience also makes us feel good when we exercise useful self-control. An attitude of "I can bear this tension for a good reason" or "I will be stronger by facing this stress" is very useful. As we control the PIG, we strengthen willpower and courage. If we give in and reinforce the PIG, it harms our lives.

b.) *Courage* is another important element of discipline because it helps to overcome unhealthy rigidities or what I call "loosen the PRUDE"--Problem of Rigid Unhealthy Disciplinary Excess. Many people, perfectionists for example, are too rigid; they find it difficult to loosen up and enjoy. For instance an anorexic patient had a rigid superego which gave extreme importance to controlling her weight, as her parents had done in her childhood. She kept her identity narrowly focused on her body image as if she were basically her body, and the social, psychological, and spiritual aspects of her life did not matter. Her extreme controls and poor nurturing had brought her close to death several times. She improved as she used her conscience and gradually loosened up her excessive control over eating and preoccupation with body image and developed more harmonious discipline, a broader identity and a deeper view of life.

c.) *Nurturing* spirit motivates us to face problems and pursue what is good. By repeatedly acting with discipline we develop good habits which are easy to maintain.

d.) *Insight and Wisdom* are also crucial parts of discipline. Insight into psychological issues and wisdom about spiritual matters help us to understand and meet our own and others' needs in healthy ways. Insight and wisdom prompt us to be pragmatic and reduce the frustrations of unmet needs by relaxation, ventilation of negative feelings, support from others, useful distractions such as hobbies, and partial satisfaction of some needs without harm.

All four of the above elements work in self-discipline as well as in disciplining others under our authority.

4. *Reassessment.* We reevaluate our decision and action based on the results of our action. Conscience promotes positive feelings if the

outcome is good and negative feelings if the outcome is bad. If we acted promptly with good intentions and failed to achieve our goal, our conscience would give us an A for effort. When we reassess, if we realize we did wrong, then conscience prompts us to repair damage and prevent repetition. That is, we use the lessons from reassessments in making future decisions.

The better we utilize these four steps, the better we live in tune with our consciences. We can remember the above four steps as ADAR and conscience as our inner RADAR.

The function of conscience itself is to judge what is right or wrong before, during, and after we act. However, good input of awareness into conscience and the output of action based on the judgment of conscience are necessary for living by one's conscience.

Psychological and spiritual growth includes increased awareness of needs, desires, patterns of thinking and behavior, opportunities for progress, and so on. Conscience actively supports and promotes increased awareness because it can function more efficiently with better information.

If we give conscience the wrong information, say for instance, that using cocaine is just pleasurable with no harm to anyone, then we are derailing its function. Even when we provide the correct information, however, our choice will not be consistent with conscience if we decide by a selfish or unfair standard. Even the correct decision will not be useful if we lack the self-discipline to act on that decision. And if we do not reassess the action based on its outcome, we miss learning from the experience and becoming wiser. Regular tuning into conscience is quite useful.

Using conscience we can also make good choices in our thinking and feeling. We can choose not to entertain bad thoughts and feelings, although all kinds of thoughts and feelings come into our minds. We can hold on to and act on thoughts and feelings that move us in the right direction. We can tune down and tune out bad thoughts and feelings.

MAKING A HABIT OF USING CONSCIENCE.

Two of the most useful of the twelve steps of Alcoholics Anonymous (AA) are taking a fearless moral inventory and taking daily moral inventory. AA's moral inventory includes recognition of good and bad intentions, thoughts, and deeds, and this helps to make better choices. Many addicts avoid taking moral inventory to evade guilt and shame about the harm they have caused by their addiction. Often, when I explain to them the function of conscience and superego and the healthy way to use guilt and shame, addicts overcome their resistance and take moral inventory.

Daily tuning in to conscience can involve paying special attention to any unhealthy habits and noting how we handle unusual incidents during the day. Assessing our choices and actions every day by the standards of conscience helps us to feel good and reinforce what is spiritually healthy. Or we may feel guilt and shame, repair damages, and avoid what is unhealthy. In doing this spiritual exercise, we must keep in mind both our tendency to distort reality and the confusion caused by superego. Usually a suitable time to take such a moral inventory is before going to sleep; if it interferes with sleep, use an earlier time.

Reassessment increases our awareness and improves our chances of making better choices in the future. The steps of conscience regarding a particular choice may stop with the reassessment. Or the reassessment may start the whole process of new awareness, followed by further decision, action, and reassessment. When we do something routinely, we may not even go through the steps of using our conscience because we have done it before. When we carry out an important task in tune with conscience, we experience joy in the effort. Then as we reassess, we rejoice if the outcome is good. Reevaluation can happen even during a course of action based on new information or undesirable consequences.

Sometimes we make a decision with limited awareness, pressured by desires or circumstances, but we realize our folly as we reevaluate the whole situation in hindsight. Then, with remorse, we correct the wrong and become wiser.

The story of Emperor Asoka (third century B.C.) is a beautiful example of great transformation resulting from reassessment and guilt about a socially admired, but destructive action. Asoka, who has been called the greatest of kings by historian H.G. Wells, was an ambitious and dynamic ruler of a vast empire that spread from Afghanistan to the southern parts of India. He invaded a small neighboring kingdom, but instead of enjoying the victory, he reflected on the immense sufferings caused by the war and regretted it deeply, and spiritually transformed his life. He embraced Buddhism and lived by its principles, including right aspiration, right mindfulness, and right effort. He organized planting of trees and medicinal herbs (some consider him the first environmentalist), provided health care for people and animals, established programs for the betterment of disadvantaged groups, and promoted the education of women. He propagated ethics in his empire and beyond. His story also shows how a major wrongdoing may stimulate growth and fulfillment of life, if we reflect, regret, and reform.

CONSCIENCE AND UNFAIR SOCIAL SYSTEMS

Some people of conscience become social activists to change unfair social systems, but such people have been rare, largely because being aware of and fighting unfair social systems are extremely difficult. If one's society claims something truly bad as good, it can mislead one's conscience to make the wrong choice unknowingly. Also, societies limit people's freedom to act.

People of good conscience, however, tend to be as fair and good as possible within the system. Once there is a move to correct an unjust system, people who are guided by their consciences tend to support the movement. But individuals guided by unfair superegos tend to be rigid and stand stubbornly to preserve the status quo. In recent history one can find numerous examples of this difference between conscience and superego when people struggled against discriminations based on caste in India and race in the United States and South Africa.

Interestingly, right-wing and left-wing extremists have one thing in common--both groups tend to deviate from conscience and do wrongs in the pursuit of their ideologies. Such extremists have resorted to killing innocent people, including children, in various parts of the world. In their avoidance or misuse of the law written in the heart, right-wing extremists tend to overplay the law and left-wing extremists overemphasize the heart. And both show high emotional attachment to their views, not using calm reflection and reason with empathy, compassion, and love. Right-wingers may keep traditions unreasonably, and left-wingers may attack traditions unnecessarily. When one side pushes too far, the other side might react more intensely.

CONFLICT AND HARMONY BETWEEN CONSCIENCE AND SUPEREGO

Many human problems--physical, social, psychological, and spiritual-- are caused by unreasonable superegos.

I see this every day. For example, Ken, who was disabled from work because of illness, became severely depressed as his superego judged and condemned him a worthless person. His depression improved greatly as he learned to judge himself by his conscience and feel good about doing his best under the circumstances.

Conscience promotes the compassionate fairness of the Golden Rule, but superego often pursues the mechanical justice of the iron rule--a tooth for a tooth--or worse. One patient expressed his modified iron rule towards another person like this: "His eight teeth for my one tooth--one tooth for compensation, two for punitive damage, one for pain and suffering, and four for my attorney."

These days, peer groups and the media greatly influence shaping of the superego. It is possible that the superego standard people learn from their families, communities, and media is the same yardstick their conscience uses, and in such cases superego and conscience give the same guidance. *For the purpose of this book, when I contrast superego and conscience, I am referring to the kind of superego that has a significantly different standard from that of conscience.*

Many or even most of the traditions, rules, laws, and manners in various cultures may be consistent with, or at least not against, the demands of conscience. So one's superego and conscience may prompt the same choices. Except when the norms of superego oppose the standards of conscience, there is no realistic reason for conflict between these two inner guides. When there is conflict, we must follow conscience, if we want to be true to our own deeper selves. As social beings, the superego has its importance in our social functioning since it helps to choose what is culturally appropriate. *Superego in tune with conscience is the ideal for social and spiritual wellness.*

The decisions of superego and conscience depend on the information they are given. Just as a computer will give the wrong result if we feed it incorrect data, our inner guides will misguide us if we give them false information. Conscience is open and eager to get correct information and gain new knowledge. But superego is resistant to information that challenges its stance. Superego also tends to view things in black and white and pushes gray areas into one or the other--often into the black area to be safer. Superego can accept what is clearly wrong as right if an accepted authority says it is right.

While conscience shows healthy flexibility, superego can be as stubborn as a mule and use asinine arguments to support its stance. The rigidity of superego depends greatly on the degree of fear or pride involved. Even when the same scare tactic is used by authorities on a group of children, some of them feel much more fear than others.

I saw this in a patient who suffered from scrupulosity (a form of Obsessive Compulsive Disorder with religiously-colored, disturbing, intrusive thoughts and compulsive acts). This man was terrified in elementary school when the nuns taught about hellfire and damnation for various sins like sexual thoughts. As an adult he was very ethical but he felt terribly guilty about even fleeting sexual thoughts or any suspicion that he had such thoughts. If he accidentally brushed against a woman's dress while walking in a hallway, he had to perform a private ritual--walk three times back and forth in the hallway without touching anyone's dress.

He used to repeat religious rituals numerous times because he was not sure that he did it right. He had a very rigid superego. He improved fast as I helped him to loosen his superego, use his conscience, and grow spiritually. This man had taken the hellfire teachings of the nuns seriously but his classmates who took it lightly did not suffer as he did.

People who have rigid superegos are too concerned about what other people, especially authorities, think of them, and they depend heavily on these others' opinions instead of on their own consciences. Their rigid, critical attitudes cause conflicts at home and at work, and their excessive guilt and shame can cause anxiety, depression, and sexual problems. Rigid superego can also cause self-hate especially when the person is down, but conscience judges with love.

Conscience stimulates guilt for wrong conduct, motivating us to repair damage and prevent repetition, but it does not promote destructive guilt. A strict superego promotes rigid discipline but a loose superego allows indiscipline and lack of appropriate guilt or shame for wrongdoing. A person guided by loose superego doesn't get enough internal pressure, if any, to transform for the better. To bring balance we can use conscience to loosen the rigid--and tighten the loose-- superego.

People of conscience prefer dialogue over proclamation, discussion instead of argument, and education as opposed to indoctrination. People guided by superego may tend to use arguments and stimulate intense feelings or stubbornness.

An anecdote about Gandhi is illustrative. At a political party meeting a member gave an emotional speech attacking Gandhi with various convoluted arguments. When the member finally finished his speech, Gandhi stood up and calmly said, "Thank you," and sat down. The audience did not need elaborate arguments to refute Gandhi's opponent.

Conscience gives great importance to sincerity, but superego is concerned about the legalistic safety of obeying the rules, crossing every "t," and dotting every "i." Conscience provides a sense of peace about doing what we sincerely consider right and doing our best. People driven by superegos do not find inner peace this way; they find peace if they feel assured that their action fits the rule book or is approved by authorities.

Many relationship problems, especially in marriage, result from the partners' different superego standards. Unreasonable superego is often behind various unhealthy relationships--be it to oneself, to others or to God. When I pointed out to a patient that he was getting increasingly sick by trying to live up to unrealistic ideals he learned from his father, his immediate reaction was: "I won't lower my standards." As I further explained to him the difference between the standard of superego and conscience and that by using conscience he would be elevating--not lowering--his standard and his life, he was able to accept the idea and make the change. Many people who grow up in dysfunctional families remain sick because their superegos perpetuate the wrong lessons they learned in childhood, but the resilient survivors follow their own consciences.

Cultures that promote too much action with too little reflection diminish the function of conscience. Reflection helps us to learn from our experiences and transform.

When conscience and superego work harmoniously, they give similar guidance, and it is hard to distinguish the one from the other. But when they are in conflict, it is not hard to see the difference. A case of Near Death Experience or NDE (people who had clinical death but returned to life shortly) beautifully illustrates the conflict between conscience and superego. Nathan had an NDE when he almost died of pneumonia in his teens. His family lived in a ghetto in New York, and his parents were poor whites who hated minorities and believed in violence and a wrathful God. Before the NDE, he was prejudiced and unfair to minorities, and fought with them frequently, and had a fanatic religious faith. He was a nervous person whose plan was to become a soldier in his family's tradition.

After the NDE, he became fair, compassionate, calm, and believed in a loving God. He gave up his prejudices and his tendency to fight. He began studying for nursing. Nathan had an inner conflict about these changes. When he was not acting mean and prejudiced as he used to do, an inner voice (superego) kept telling him he was doing wrong. At the same time, deep within him, another voice (conscience) kept telling him that he was doing right. He continued to live by his conscience and slowly his superego quit troubling him.

The following table summarizes superego and conscience:

SUPEREGO	CONSCIENCE
Formed by internalized values of good and bad from family and society	Innate human capacity to judge good and bad using reason and the Golden Rule
Good is what family and society teach as good	Good is what is good for oneself and fair to others
Motivated by fear of punishment or hope of reward	Motivated by reason and love, compassion or fairness
Approval of others very important	Approval of one's deeper self is more important
Tends to be rather a closed system; resistant to change	Flexible and open to change based on reason and fairness
Takes a narrow view of the situation	Takes a broad view of the situation
Too much emotional attachment to its stance	Less emotional, more rational and open
Superego's stance rationalized; healthy skepticism not used	Stance not rationalized; healthy skepticism is used
May appear very consistent because of stubbornness	May appear inconsistent but shows consistency of goodness
Much importance given to the letter of the laws	Importance is given to the spirit of the laws
Tends to foster legalism	Discourages legalism

Wrongdoing causes excessive or inadequate guilt or shame	Wrongdoing causes appropriate and useful guilt or shame
Excessively defensive	Not excessively defensive
Takes too much blame on self or shifts blame to others	Puts blame where it belongs--on self or others
Tries unrealistic solutions	Realistic solutions tried
Information that challenges superego's position rejected without due consideration	Any important information is given due consideration
Discipline of self and others is excessive or inadequate	Discipline of self and others is adequate and balanced
Oriented to authority figures	Oriented to reason, fairness
Past wrongs are remembered to beat oneself or forgotten without learning from it	Past wrongs are evaluated and wisdom from the experience, not bad feelings, is kept
Comparison to others is used excessively for criticism or approval of self	Comparison to others used to learn useful matters and enhance love and wisdom

THE ASTOUNDING POWER AND BENEFITS OF CONSCIENCE

- Conscience, which is both nurturing and protective, is within us, so we can easily utilize it.
- Conscience is the key to spiritual strength.
- Conscience and virtue go hand in hand.
- Conscientious individuals live longer, as shown by a seventy-year follow-up study of over 1,500 people.[15]
- Conscience can be an extremely powerful element of psychological health.
- Living by a well-informed conscience promotes inner tranquillity, discipline, and happy relationships.
- Seven of the twelve steps of AA and similar groups are about ways to use conscience in making right choices.
- Healthy conscience is the most significant feature of the strong survivors of dysfunctional families.
- Mahatma Gandhi and others who used his approach

transformed individuals, communities, and nations for the better by using the power of conscience.

- Conscience and courage were the main features of the ordinary people who saved Jews from Hitler.[16]

To live by our consciences and enjoy fulfilling lives, we have to avoid the self-defeating games we tend to play to evade and misuse conscience, our next topic.

3. Stop Self-Defeating Games

"If you want to slip into a round hole, you must make a ball of yourself.[17]"

George Eliot

"...once the angel in us is repressed it turns into a demon."[18]

Viktor Frankl

In trying to meet our needs in sneaky ways we tend to play games with our consciences and end up harming ourselves and others. *We con our consciences at the risk of damaging our own fulfillment.* To explain this issue I often use the story of *Dr. Jekyll and Mr. Hyde* by Robert Louis Stevenson.

Dr. Jekyll was basically a good person, a physician who worked hard to relieve people's suffering. He was well respected and carried his head high. He desired some undignified pleasures (Stevenson does not specify what   pleasures), but he concealed this desire because it was beneath his unusually high ideals. He found a clever solution to the conflict between his high ideals and his need for the undignified pleasures: he concocted a potion that temporarily changed him into Mr. Hyde, thus allowing him to enjoy the secret pleasures while still preserving Jekyll's lofty image. This dubious solution to meeting his conflicting needs became his worst problem. The trouble was that Hyde gradually became increasingly powerful, and at his hands the merely undignified pleasures of Jekyll became human monstrosities, including murder. The story ends with Jekyll's tragic death from excessively drinking the potion.

Jekyll confesses that he was shocked by Hyde's actions at times but the strange situation had "insidiously *relaxed the grasp of conscience. It was Hyde and Hyde alone that was guilty. Jekyll was no worse; he woke again to his good qualities seemingly unimpaired; he would even make haste, where it was possible, to undo the evil done by Hyde. And thus his conscience slumbered*" (italics added).[19]

Jekyll knew about Hyde's evils and hastily tried to undo some of them, but he did not use his conscience and reevaluate his pattern of meeting his needs for pleasure and esteem. Jekyll used what I call a "spiritual defense," something we more or less consciously do to hoodwink or deaden conscience. Jekyll could have faced his inner conflict head on rather than deadening his conscience. He could have brought his too high ideal, his superego, down to a more realistic level. Or he could have denied his desire for the undignified pleasures and used other enjoyments acceptable to his ideals. He could have gained the support of his conscience for either of these choices, but *he chose to keep conning his own conscience which inevitably led him to a tragic end.*

When we use spiritual defenses, we have some awareness of doing wrong, but we block the operation of conscience and thereby avoid guilt, shame, or anxiety. It is like taking the battery out of the fire alarm because we dislike the sound of the alarm, thus risking getting burnt.

If Dr. Jekyll had Multiple Personality Disorder and had *unconsciously* switched to an altered personality, he would have been using a psychological defense called *dissociation.* Psychological defenses are *unconscious;* they tune down feelings and buy time to adjust to big changes, thereby reducing the inner stress caused by our internal and external demands. We are not morally responsible for our psychological defenses since they operate unconsciously. We are, however, responsible for our spiritual defenses since we are more or less aware of what we are doing.

Psychological defenses are like a problem we do not see, but spiritual defenses are like a problem we see but we avert our eyes and act as if we do not see it because we do not want to deal with it.

In order to make good choices, it is crucial to know about psychological and spiritual defenses. Since numerous books have discussed psychological defenses, I won't go into the same here, but information about them is provided in the appendix. Here I will focus on three points about psychological defenses from a spiritual angle.

First, the psychological defense of denial is *unconsciously* refusing to accept an unwanted piece of information. Although in a psychotic condition people use denial, drug addicts and people with personality disorders are often *consciously* denying or lying and not using the unconscious defense. Or they may be "bullshitting" as described by Harry G Frankfurt in *On Bullshit*. Unlike the liar, the bullshitter is indifferent to the truth and misrepresents his or her agenda by making things up or cleverly picking things here and there. Frakfurt asserts: "...bullshit is a greater enemy of the truth than lies are."[20]

Second, sublimation as a psychological defense can be easily misunderstood. Sublimation is a substitute activity that meets instinctual needs. If a man had urges to attack others with a knife earlier in his life and he became a surgeon instead of a criminal, it would be an example of sublimation. But it would be a gross mistake to think of all or most surgery as sublimation of aggressive impulse. There have been strange interpretations of paintings as sublimation of smearing feces and organ music as sublimation of farting.

Third, some authors since Freud have included altruism and humor as psychological defenses. Altruism is an active regard for the needs of others. Humor is the capacity to feel or stimulate amusement. From a spiritual point of view, altruism is not a defense but an essential part of a healthy lifestyle based on spiritual values of compassion and love.

Humor may be a cover up for something else at times, but usually it is a form of intellectual pleasure. A good sense of humor is natural to spiritual people because of their gentle and broad outlook on life. In contrast, sarcasm, which comes from the Greek word *sarkazien*--"to tear flesh like dogs"--often hides hostility. Not surprisingly, sarcasm is popular in the world of dog-eat-dog competition.

Humor can also help to gently confront another person's spiritual defense. For instance, a supporter of Lord Irwin, a British viceroy to India, once told Gandhi that the viceroy always made decisions only after praying about it. After reflecting briefly, Gandhi replied: "And why do you suppose that God so consistently gives him wrong advice?"

SPIRITUAL DEFENSES

Spiritual defenses make us feel comfortable by evading conscience, but it is a self-defeating, often destructive, game. We diminish or even destroy ourselves by such defenses in the long run. In the short run, though, we get certain pleasure and profit from meeting our needs in ways that would cause bad feelings if we used our consciences. Unreasonable religious rules and cultural ideals can even pressure one's superego to reject desires or feelings which are healthy or acceptable to conscience. Then the person might meet the need in harmful ways, as Dr. Jekyll did. Another example is a woman whose ideals prohibited her from showing anger or talking about it. When she was angry with her husband, she relieved her frustration by retaliation--withholding sex for weeks. With therapy she realized this problem and learned to talk to her husband about her anger and resolve it easily.

Many religious people talk about the conflict between the spirit and the flesh, and some take this idea to the extreme by rejecting sensual pleasures or even inflicting pain on themselves. But healthy spirituality opposes such extremism and celebrates the enjoyment of pleasures consistent with conscience. Many of our conflicts with our spiritual part are not due to our physical needs but due to our psychological needs to be successful and respected members of our social groups by using wrong means. Dr. Jekyll's desire for keeping a lofty image was a bigger problem for him than his desire for pleasure. Jekyll confesses that many men would have even proudly proclaimed the pleasure he was enjoying, but he regarded it with intense shame because of his ideals. "It was thus rather the exacting nature of my aspirations than any particular degradation in my faults, that made me what I was...."[21]

The Importance of Psychological and Spiritual Defenses

Since psychological defenses are unconscious, the most important step in dealing with them is to become conscious of them. We can become conscious of our psychological defenses by four approaches: insight oriented psychotherapy, psychological tests such as the Minnesota Multiphasic Personality Inventory, by learning about psychological defenses and using that knowledge to examine our pattern of behavior, and listening to useful feedback from others. As we become aware of our defenses, we can put our energies into transformation. For instance, if your family and friends tell you that you act childishly under much stress, you can take a serious look at whether you are using the defense of regression and, if so, choose better ways of dealing with stress.

Since we have some awareness of our wrong choice behind the smoke screen of spiritual defense, the major step here is to use that awareness with compassion and love. The compassion and love keep guilt and shame at useful levels, help us to face our wrongs, and take corrective steps. We can feel good about recognizing and doing the right thing. The better our understanding of human needs the more our ability to recognize and deal with our defenses. Defenses are ways to meet certain needs. If we have a habit of using certain defenses, we can be realistic about needing time, patience, and persistence to change the habit.

Substance abusers and people with Personality Disorders use excessive psychological defenses. In my experience, they use a great deal of spiritual defenses too. They consciously lie and manipulate to get what they want. A major benefit of the spirituality of AA for alcoholics is that it helps them cut through spiritual defenses and use conscience.

Similarly, in treating personality disorders (persistent pattern of maladaptive behaviors), I find it very beneficial to discuss with them the healthy ways to use conscience and point out how they evade conscience by their spiritual defenses. A patient with Hysterical Personality Disorder used to exaggerate facts and figures and stir up her feelings way out of proportion to many situations. Although she gained attention and some power by such behaviors, it caused her serious problems at home and at work. She was conscious of her manipulations, but she evaded her conscience by focusing on her feelings and acting on them without judging whether her choices were good or bad. As I pointed out these tendencies to her, she learned to tune down her feelings and live by her conscience. Then she became happy with her job and her relationships.

By its loving and compassionate judgment, conscience makes it far easier to admit a problem to oneself. But a harsh superego makes it very difficult to admit one's faults, and a loose superego doesn't protest enough against irrational gratification and selfishness. Families and societies with rigid and too high ideals make it hard for people to admit frailties and overcome them. Conversely, very permissive groups approve doing what feels good without using one's conscience.

PATTERNS OF SPIRITUAL DEFENSES

After doing wrong or as they plan to do wrong, many people evade guilt and shame by five common methods: neutralizing guilt/shame by wrong arguments, replacing the standard of conscience with self-serving ideals, focusing on the execution of the action without reflecting on whether it is good or bad, using false appeals to virtue, and getting support from others for doing the wrong. As I was writing this book and I was reading some parts of Shakespeare, I was totally amazed to find all these five methods presented just in five lines in *King Richard III*. After being torn by guilt about the murders and treason he had committed, the king says:

Conscience is but a word that cowards use,

Devis'd at first to keep the strong in awe:

Our strong arms be our conscience, swords our law.

March on, join bravely, let us to't pell-mell:

If not to heaven, then hand in hand to hell.

The king neutralizes his guilt by arguing that conscience is for cowards, implying that he, being brave, doesn't have to use conscience, and his guilt was a false alarm he could ignore. Using our reasoning ability to make an angle of argument for unfair gain or shifting blame is a common problem. Conscience needs the input of a broad perspective, not an angle of argument or a spin. But superego is fond of arguments to support its stance. In trying to win an argument, some people take the opponent's view to an extreme and make it appear worse than it really is. Those who argue a lot from one angle without considering the overall perspective are likely guided by superego and not conscience. A culture of arguments and spins overlooking the broad picture promotes spiritual defenses, not spirituality.

Next, the king replaces the standard of conscience with a "might is right" philosophy of strong arms and swords. Many social groups idealize the selfish use of power and force. Their Golden Rule seems to be that those who have more gold rule. Some people use Charles Darwin's theory of evolution to promote the so-called Social Darwinism which was not Darwin's idea, but that of some of his followers, especially Herbert Spencer. Social Darwinism promotes the idea of survival of the fittest in human relationships. Spencer opposed charity for the poor; the weak were to be left to perish. Thus, social Darwinism is a selfish *ideology* contrary to conscience, not a scientific theory.

Then, the king falsely appeals to the virtue of bravery; true courage would have made them face their evil deeds. Extremists often falsely appeal to virtues such as loyalty, courage, and love of God to promote evil deeds by their followers. Many religious extremists destroy others in the name of God. In *The Merchant of Venice* Shakespeare observes: "The devil can cite scripture for his purpose." Promoting vices in the name of virtues is a particularly clever ploy to fool conscience.

The king's next trick is focusing on action without further reflection on his evil deeds. Excessive doing without using the evaluation of conscience can do us in spiritually. Cultures that are heavily action-oriented with little reflection promote superficiality in understanding which constricts the function of conscience.

The last method the king uses is group support for his wrong doings. Such external support of others relieves the internal pressure of guilt and shame. And the group's ideology becomes part of the person's superego which can shout down the still small voice of conscience. Gangs, cults, and groups of religious and ideological extremists use group support to deaden their consciences. Many people who were members of such groups have told me that their initial prick of conscience about the groups' values disappeared as they got more indoctrinated by the group. On the other hand, the twelve step programs and healthy spiritual groups stimulate and strengthen conscience. A minister's wife told me how a woman in their congregation used to gather a click and stimulate feelings against the minister instead of discussing her issues directly with him.

One method that King Richard doesn't use but that is often used by many people to deaden their conscience is alcohol and drug abuse. There is an old saying that alcohol dissolves conscience. The English word "assassin" originated from an Arabic word "hashshashin" meaning hashish smokers--a group of Islamic fanatics who used to smoke hashish before secretly murdering people they considered their enemies. Substance abuse stimulates the problem of irrational gratification--the PIG--and loosens the control of conscience at the same time, thereby doubling evil tendencies. Add group support to that and you can imagine the resulting dynamics of destructiveness.

One can interfere and distort the function of conscience at every step of its operation: awareness, decision, action, and reevaluation. Let us look at the way conscience is misused or evaded at each of these steps.

AWARENESS

As we saw in the previous chapter, our awareness may be from external sources like seeing a dangerous situation, or from internal sources such as feeling guilty. Awareness comes from perceptions, feelings, and knowledge. All our five senses provide us with information about the possibility, or even the urgency, of meeting certain needs. In using our senses, we often choose what we pay attention to, depending on what is important to us for healthy or unhealthy reasons. For healthy reasons, a compassionate person may notice another's subtle distress and help that individual, whereas self-centered people may not even notice the person's distress. For unhealthy reasons, a criminal may see hidden opportunities to exploit someone in a crisis.

Feelings are very important sources of awareness, but they can give us right or wrong, accurate or highly inaccurate, signals. Take anger, for instance. A man who was sexually abused in childhood tended to be extremely angry with his wife and verbally abused her if she did not follow his wishes, especially sexually. He took a "no" from her as a personal rejection and punishment and felt it necessary to retaliate with criticism and contempt. His superego agreed with his reaction, and so he felt justified about his angry outbursts. His wife had to pressure him hard to take a look at this problem because he was not aware of how he was destroying his relationship with her. In therapy he learned that his anger towards his wife was based on his mistaken sense of rejection by her, and that his verbal abuse of her was wrong and self-defeating. He learned to understand the sources of his feelings and use his conscience in choosing his actions; so he overcame his problem.

An awareness of our own and others' needs, and an understanding of the healthy and unhealthy ways we humans deal with our needs is extremely useful. Just as we can utilize the technical knowledge available to us, without having to reinvent the wheel, we can use psychological, social, and religious knowledge available to us. Excess or deficiency of feelings, rigid superego or ideology, and poor knowledge about human needs greatly diminish our awareness.

If feelings are excessive, our overall awareness gets distorted. For example, if we strongly dislike a person, we are less likely to notice the good qualities and more apt to recognize the bad qualities of that individual.

Deficiency of feelings also causes distorted awareness. For instance, if we don't have tender feelings, we may not sense how our criticism would hurt somebody. Compassionate and loving feelings keep our soul energized. In sharp contrast to the idea that strong men don't cry, Victor Hugo observed that dry eyes belong to a dead soul[22]. Men who cry at really sad occasions are truly strong, not weak.

Many groups tend not to deal with negative feelings. Stephen Arterburn and Jack Felton note this tendency in toxic faith systems: "Be it the church of the 'frozen chosen' or the church of the 'eternal smile,' certain feelings aren't allowed.... Toxic faith parents and leaders of organizations don't want to face the reality of human needs.... They want to live in a world where everything can be fixed with a great sermon or a quick prayer."[23]

The more we know about our choices and the benefits and problems of each choice, the better input we provide our consciences to make the right choice. That brings us to how we play games with the next step of conscience--decision.

DECISION

In the decision-making stage the game people play is not applying the standards of conscience--doing what is useful and not harmful for oneself in the long run, and what is fair and responsible to others. Instead, various other standards or values--religious, cultural, or other group values or personal ideology that contradict conscience--are used. Thus, exploitation of women, children, slaves, lower castes, colonial subjects, and the like have been given religious or cultural sanctions. When they go against conscience, religious groups use various arguments based on their doctrines or traditions, without sincerely applying the ethical spirit of their faiths with a broad perspective. Terrorism has been sanctioned by several religious and ideological groups in different parts of the world. I want to emphasize here that, on their healthy side, religions and cultures stimulate and strengthen conscience.

Another false philosophy of life is traditionalism--taking a tradition to unhealthy extremes. Tradition gives people certain guidelines for action in various situations, especially when going through important stages of life such as birth, marriage, and death. Tradition reduces the stress of having to analyze and discover one's own approach to dealing with many challenging situations in life.

Traditions can enhance harmony within society. As the hero of the movie *Fiddler on the Roof* demonstrates, tradition had taught him what to do or not to do in many situations, but he was knocked for a loop when he faced situations that did not fit traditional patterns. When his three daughters deviated from tradition in their choice of mates, he was torn between his love for his daughters and his attachment to tradition. Although he was willing to deviate some from his tradition, he was scared stiff that if he bent too far, it would break the back of his faith and destroy him. Traditions are useful in many ways, but if taken to extremes, they become more perdition than solution.

There is often confusion between tradition and values. Many different values may be connected with a tradition, and some of those values may be healthy while others may be troublesome. For instance, the tradition of individualism includes both the healthy value of personal responsibility and the unhealthy value of isolationism. Psychologist Martin Seligman has observed that rampant individualism causes depression and meaninglessness.[24] Moderation is needed in traditions too.

In much the same way, "Cultism" or excessive fusion with a group damages authentic decision making. In merging too intensely with the group (be it cult, religion, or nation) people give up their true individuality and follow the group's ideology, even against conscience.

Excessive dependence on authority figures or blind belief in their teachings is another common defense that protects people from facing their own freedom and responsibility to be authentic. The authority may be a group, a tradition, or a person. Authoritarianism has become less in our democratic age, but it is prevalent among rigid religious and social groups. Healthy respect for wise leaders is based on good reasons and not blind faith.

Since I mentioned faith many times, I want to stress that I am not opposed to the leap of faith that is relevant in spirituality. But I believe we ought to look carefully before we leap and after we land to keep a healthy balance.

In spiritual egocentrism the person uses religious or ideological rationale to foster a very self-centered lifestyle. One woman's husband, a minister, persuaded her to abuse drugs and have group sex with him by using two arguments. First, she should obey him as the Bible teaches wives to do, and secondly, since they had been saved, they could sin without the fear of eternal damnation.

Manipulative skepticism is a cunning method some people use to derail good reasoning in making decisions. It is different from genuine doubt. When a matter is unclear, we naturally have questions and doubts, but in manipulative skepticism the individual uses various arguments to suit a selfish purpose. Manipulative skeptics are eager to find some argument or loophole so they can do what they selfishly desire. They are not open to the truth. Many addicts, for instance, would bring up various doubts and arguments to deny or minimize their problem and the need for treatment.

ACTION

Once the conscience makes the decision the next step is action. Procrastination and inaction are potential problems here, and both of these problems involve deficiency of self-discipline. Also, conscience has to be alert to notice whether the decision was correct on the basis of ongoing experience. Suppose we started doing something with the intention of helping someone, but as we proceeded, we noticed that our effort was hurting the person; then we have to stop and reevaluate the situation instead of staying the course.

If doing what is good brings joy, then it reinforces continuation of the behavior. The greater the difficulty of the task we are engaged in, the better the appreciation from our conscience we receive for our effort. Then the next step of reevaluation can bring much more joy.

REASSESSMENT

The judgment of conscience in reevaluating our action in the light of its results is extremely important. Based on this judgment we may rejoice or regret our action, and we may decide to repeat or refrain from similar action in the future. Many people do not reevaluate their actions, especially if the outcome of the action is bad. Typically, individuals with personality disorders tend to blame others or circumstances in their lives for their wrongdoing.

The transformation of Jean Val Jean, emperor Asoka and many others we have seen resulted from them reevaluating their wrongs, repenting, and changing for the better. Religions often advocate that people repent their sins, leave evil ways, and do good. Greek poet Sophocles observed in *Antigone* that it is human to err and only those who do not repent and repair are condemned.

Spiritual defenses have strong group influence and support-- often exerted through superego--which make it more difficult for the individual to transform. Like a child who is given a pacifier too often instead of nutrition, the person who uses excessive defenses remains weak and unfulfilled--even destructive. Healthy use of conscience is obviously the solution to this problem. Certain levels of psychological defenses are useful to manage high stresses of life. When these defenses are excessive, they cause psychiatric symptoms or problems with work or relationships. People guided by enlightened consciences would notice such problems and take actions to remedy them.

Socrates asserted that an unexamined life is not worth living. A way of life unexamined by conscience is not a worthy choice because it tragically misses the opportunity to live an authentically fulfilling life.

4. GET A PERSPECTIVE ON NEEDS

"To be strong, a person must acquire frustration tolerance,... the ability to love others and to enjoy their need-gratification as well as one's own (not to use other people only as means)."[25]
Abraham Maslow

Understanding each of our needs and putting them in perspective will enable us to deal with them in fulfilling ways. Let us look at our various needs and some important common features about them.

HUMAN NEEDS

1. *Physical/biological needs and sexuality.* Air, water, food, shelter, sleep, and elimination of waste are obviously the basic needs for human survival. Safety and avoidance of pain, stimulation and activity, and sex are other biological needs. But sexuality is far more than just a biological need; it has a strong impact on all needs.

2. *Esteem and value.* As creatures who judge ourselves, we have a need to feel good about ourselves or to have good self-esteem. Also, we have a need to feel good about how others judge us, the need for esteem from others. We need values not only for judging ourselves and others but also for establishing standards by which to live.

3. *Identity.* We need a sense of who we are and how we fit into the larger schemes of life.

4. *Relationships.* We have a need to relate to ourselves, other people and beings, the universe and the infinite.

5. *Meaning.* We have a strong need for meaning in life.

6. *Power and freedom.* We need the power to meet our needs, a sense of security from external and internal threats against our wellness, and freedom to make choices.

7. *Integrating the past.* Since we have long-term memory and judge our actions and experiences, we have a need to be at peace with our past or integrate our past.

8. *Present balance and future direction.* We need a balance in the various forces affecting us at the present time. And we need a sense of direction in life involving both immediate and long-term future, including death.

9. *Comfort and pleasure.* It is not enough for us just to survive; we need comfort and pleasure.

An activity such as work is extremely important because it is connected with meeting biological needs as well as power, esteem, identity, relationships, meaning, and pleasure. Therefore, job insecurity can undermine the various needs related to work and cause intense distress.

Meeting Needs with Love and Wisdom

We can meet our needs lovingly, in creative ways that fulfill ourselves and others. For example, a loving husband meets his need for intimacy and sexual pleasure by having mutually satisfactory intimacy and sex with his wife. But a selfish husband may meet his needs for intimacy and sex by demands, threats, or guilt trips, disregarding his wife's needs.

Finally, a sex abuser may hatefully meet his sexual and aggressive needs by forcing sexual acts on his victims.

Happy relationships provide an excellent example of meeting needs lovingly. Tolstoy observed that happy families resemble one another; the resemblance I notice is that members of happy families help meet each other's needs.

Conversely, unmet needs underlie relationship conflicts. A workaholic husband who has a strong need for financial security has perpetual conflict with his wife whose strong need is for pleasure, especially the need for romantic companionship. If they understood the differences in each other's needs and accommodated them with a loving spirit, the relationship would be happy. Although the husband was financially successful, he was not really happy, and his wife was depressed; regrettably, he refused to consider any change on his part that would make both his wife's and his own life happy. He saw her depression as her problem that she and her doctor should fix; thus, they lived miserably.

Love varies in intensity depending on the object of our love. In close relationships, the level of nurturing and protection of the ones we love is high. But in distant or strained relationships, we can at least use our conscience and be fair and reasonable rather than hateful to the others. We need wisdom to understand and practice these different aspects of love.

Wisdom involves knowledge, broad perspective, openness of mind, and practical understanding and interest in the deeper aspects of life. I have been amazed at the wisdom of many people in different cultures in spite of their very limited education. They showed broad perspective, openness of mind, practical understanding, and interest in the deeper aspects of life. While ignorant of psychological theories, such people of wisdom were psychologically minded because of their open-mindedness and deeper interest.

We manifest love and wisdom in the ways we deal with our own and others' needs. A great deal of confusion and conflicts in human relationships is caused by three differences in needs among people--differences in priority, intensity, and in the way of dealing with needs.

As noted in the Introduction, people have different priorities in their needs; one person's priority may be pleasure and another's power. Also, priorities can change at different times and stages of life. Gaining financial power by acquiring a good job may be the most important need for someone at one stage, but later the priority may be to find a life companion.

Many misunderstandings are caused by differences in the intensity of needs. People with very low sexual desire often find it hard to understand--in fact they may actively misunderstand--the high sex drive of their partners. A wife with low sexual desire told me: "I think my husband just loves my butt, and not me." He really loved her and showed it by his devotion and commitment. So, I posed her a question: "If your husband needs twice as much food as you need and he asks for second helpings would you feel like he is only interested in your cooking and not in you?" I did not imply that making love more often is as simple as providing extra food, and the woman understood my point about how she was misinterpreting her husband's sex drive.

Given the importance as well as the individual variations of human needs, I propose the following rule.

The Golden Rule of Needs: *Value the importance of other peoples' needs for them as you value your needs for yourself. But do not try to meet their needs how you meet yours, for they may prefer to meet their needs differently.*

Recognize that other people may be quite different from you in their priority, intensity, and method of need-satisfaction. One person meets the need for self-esteem by acquiring wealth and another meets it by helping others.

We tend to put other people in our shoes. True empathy is a wonderful quality, but the superficial attitude of "Only this worked for me and so only this particular approach will work for anybody" is quite incorrect. It would be like saying "only this shoe fits me and so I know only this size shoe would fit anybody." The deeper spirit of the Golden

Rule is letting others meet their needs based on   priorities and means that are most suitable to them.

PROTECT AND NURTURE YOUR NEED SATISFACTION

Every human need has both a nurturing and a protective aspect, which means that we put time and energy into two channels. In the case of power, we try to nurture our power by using our abilities in healthy ways, and we attempt to protect our power from damage by others exploiting us. So, our energies go into two channels. If we use unnecessary amount of energy to protect our power, for example by overreacting to reasonable competition from others, we waste some of our resources, and we may reinforce even more undesirable competition from others.

The healthy proportion of protection to nurturing is well illustrated by an analogy to a fruit. Each fruit has a protective skin and nurturing fleshy parts and seeds. The best fruit has a minimum amount of skin and maximum amount of flesh and desirable amount of seeds. The coconut is an example of a fruit with a very strong protective part, a thick fibrous husk and a hard shell, which protect the fruit from damage when it falls from the coconut tree or when it is carried by water and deposited in water-soaked ground where it can sprout and grow. For the coconut, the amount of resource going into the protective side is appropriate. Inside the hard shell is the coconut's meat and the embryo. There are malformed coconuts that look normal and have the usual husk and the shell but no meat or embryo inside. It is as if the resources of these coconuts have gone completely into protecting, but protecting nothing; the result is empty nuts.

People can also waste their resources in unnecessary protection. The key is to use our time and energy to develop and maintain minimum necessary defenses and maximum nurturing. This basic principle applies also to societies and nations. As historian Paul Kennedy points out in *The Rise and Fall of Great Powers*, spending too much on military defenses can bring down prosperity and the power itself of powerful nations.[26] One of the causes for the fall of the Soviet Union, for instance, was excessive military expenditure.

An example of excessive defensiveness involves two brothers who grew up in a dysfunctional family. When they were children, their mother's mental condition was unstable. The family moved several times and had financial problems. The parents divorced when the children were preschoolers. The older brother became aggressive, easily offended, and very defensive. He has had problems in relationships because of his aggressive and intimidating ways to others for even minor conflicts. On the other hand, the younger brother became nurturing. He has many close friends, a steady girlfriend, several hobbies, a good job, and has helped his mother to stay on medication.

In both protecting and in nurturing our needs, our feelings, thoughts, and actions are involved. In order to fulfill our needs and be happy, we have to channel our feelings, thoughts, and actions in a healthy direction.

FEELINGS

Our feelings, which are closely tied to our needs, have four functions: to give signals, provide motivation, generate pleasant or unpleasant sensations or moods, and help modulate relationships.

1. *Feelings as signals.* Feelings such as guilt, fear, or desire alert us to internal needs, external threats, or opportunities to meet a need. For instance, guilt signals wrong doing, fear signals danger and lustful feelings alert us to opportunities for sexual gratification. The signals we receive from our feelings may be correct or incorrect, and if they continue when they have no further purpose to serve, they become nuisances, like an alarm clock that we did not shut off after it woke us up.

2. *Feelings as motivating forces.* Feelings or emotions often move us to act, and strong feelings can motivate us to act forcefully. Healthy

guilt coming from an individual's conscience can motivate the person to make amends and take steps to prevent repetition of the wrong. Anger about being treated unfairly can motivate us to confront the situation and bring about fairness or leave the situation. Fear can motivate us to take healthy protective steps.

But feelings can also work against our best interests by causing the wrong motivation or taking away useful motivation. For example, excessive fear can cause people to restrict their choices too much or to freeze in a dangerous situation when defensive action is necessary for survival. Moreover, excessive guilt that causes depression may motivate self-destructive actions or no action at all.

Motivating feelings may also cause harm by overshooting the mark. For instance, the pleasurable feeling from drinking alcohol motivates a person to have one drink, but that doesn't satisfy the need for pleasure, so the person continues to drink and risks injuring self and others.

3. *Feelings as pleasant or unpleasant sensations and moods.* Good feelings and pleasure or bad feelings and discomfort go hand in hand; so it is healthy to let go of painful feelings and hold on to pleasant feelings. Practices such as meditation and visualization help in developing the ability to let go or keep certain feelings or thoughts.

Feelings such as excitement, relief, and enjoyment create good moods, while feelings such as frustration, sadness, and anger create bad moods. And moods influence feelings. That is, if we are already in a bad mood when something disappointing happens, we are likely to experience more frustration than if we were in a good mood.

4. *Feelings modulate relationships.* Our feelings toward somebody or something influence how we relate to that person or circumstance. Our feelings toward others depend on several factors: our previous experience with the person and similar people, our expectations and needs, the other person's actions and reactions, and so on. Based on our overall feelings, we keep varying degrees of closeness or distance.

However, unless we are aware of the real reasons for our feelings we can make big mistakes in relationships. For instance, we may feel cozy toward con artists based on their charming ways, only to be unpleasantly surprised by their deception later. We must be careful to relate to others based on the reality of the situation, rather than just our feelings.

We tend to create, exaggerate, or minimize feelings for our purpose. Just as we use our imagination to calm down or to get excited, we can use our imagination to stir up anger, hurt, or other feelings so that we can manipulate others for our purpose. We can even just *pretend* we are feeling a certain way. In other words, some people pitch fits to get their way, and others act hurt to stimulate compassion. Sometimes pretending to feel a particular way may be useful and fair, but often it is not.

FEELINGS AND THOUGHTS

Thoughts can evoke feelings, or we may get feelings before we get thoughts. We may remember and think about something scary that happened and feel anxious. Or we may get a feeling of anxiety and then have scary thoughts about something dangerous. No matter which comes first, feelings and thoughts go together, and strong feelings cause physical as well as mental reactions.

We have most control over our actions, less over our thoughts, and least over our feelings. But we can use our thoughts to control feelings. For example, say you feel angry thinking about an incident when someone hurt your pride and you want to take revenge. As long as your thoughts are focused on the hurt and wanting revenge, you are likely to have angry feelings. But if you change your thoughts to how unimportant the incident was in the overall scheme of life and how great it is to let such things go, your feelings of anger would diminish and gradually disappear.

HEALTHY THINKING

Healthy thinking is rational, open-minded, based on broad perspective, and pragmatic. Excessive feelings and defenses distort our thinking. One common irrational pattern of thinking is the either/or mentality in which everything tends to be seen in polar opposites: superior or inferior, smart or dumb, friend or foe, etc. Gray areas get pushed into one or the other extreme.

The all-or-nothing approach is a variation of the either/or mentality. For instance, some people judge themselves as failures because they did not achieve their goals exactly as they planned even though they have tried hard and have done fairly well.

Overgeneralization is another irrational pattern of thinking. Here a person jumps into unrealistic conclusions based on very limited information. Specifically, people who were badly hurt in close relationships may avoid intimacy because of unrealistic fears beyond reasonable caution.

Drawing wrong conclusions about other people's motives is another common form of irrational thinking. If we do not get input from the person and give it due consideration, we are likely to form the wrong opinion. Someone once said that to assume (ass-u-me) is to make an ass of you and me.

Next, we often use certain prejudiced notions in judging. "Prejudice," as the word suggests, is judging devoid of proper reasoning, without utilizing relevant facts and figures. We pick up many prejudices from social groups, and often make rash judgments without using our consciences.

Open-mindedness helps to prevent prejudging. Open-mindedness is the willingness to play along with an idea long enough to understand it before making judgment about it. It is not accepting everything--that would be a hole in the head rather than an open-mind. If we are too emotional about something, our mind tends to be closed on that matter. Such close-mindedness can lead to extremism.

Superficiality is a common problem in thinking. Unlike the old saying not to "judge a book by its cover," recent trends driven by slick advertisements are to judge by superficial features. Real wisdom in any age involves the capacity to go beyond fashions and fads and view matters in the broad perspective of life.

When we view matters with an open mind and relevant information, we gain a broad perspective. Relevant information includes the wisdom of our culture, at least some basic psychological insights, and useful ideas from other cultures. If our attention is too focused on one need or just on the daily routines, we are likely to miss a broad perspective. As a Chassidic proverb says, "Just as the hand, held before the eye, can hide the tallest mountain, so the routine of everyday life can keep us from seeing the vast radiance and the secret wonders that fill the world."

Each culture teaches its members the priority of needs and wants and how to meet them. Sometimes the culture sends mixed or contradictory messages, and what is expected of men and women may be significantly different. Many cultures today teach women that body image is extremely important, and many women who are mildly overweight have seriously low self-esteem because they fall short of the ideal of being slim. That is, their extra weight weighs heavier on their minds than on their bodies. For men, achievement is the main source of esteem in many cultures. In general, members of different societies tend to be more competitive or more cooperative depending on what each society promotes.

Wants are our conscious desires or wishes, and there is a need behind each want. Often our wants are conditioned by ideas we learn from our culture, and it may not be what we really need. Also, sometimes getting what we want may not satisfy our need. The real need is what is truly important.

To illustrate, Lila, a neglected teenage girl from a dysfunctional family, *wanted* badly to have a child because she felt she would be happy if she had a child she could love and care for and who would love her in return. In reality, Lila was not ready for the serious responsibilities and stresses of parenthood. Instead, what Lila needed was to love herself and others already in her life, and grow up so that she could become a happy mother one day.

Misunderstanding our own and others' needs causes considerable conflicts and suffering. This is what happened when Janice arranged a surprise birthday party for her husband, James. Janice had grown up in a family that placed a strong priority on celebrating birthdays and other occasions, but in James's family paying bills on time was the top priority, and celebrations were unimportant. Janice and James were having financial difficulties, and James was worried about some bills. Janice had saved up some money, and she assumed that James would accept and enjoy if she used it for his birthday party. But James got angry, and after the guests left that evening, the couple had a big fight. Discussing the incident later in therapy, they realized the differences in their priorities of needs. These insights helped them to meet each other's needs much better.

Therefore, opening our minds and seeking to understand others will help us recognize and meet each other's unmet needs. While psychological and spiritual defense mechanisms distort our vision and cause confusion, when we relate to others in a cooperative and creative mode with open ears, eyes, and minds, we can get a much truer picture of them than if we have defensive or hateful attitudes. In short, we tend to misinterpret others' needs in ways favorable to what we want. Likewise, people with excessive guilt or shame tend to interpret their own actions unfavorably and perpetuate bad feelings about themselves.

ACTIONS

Correct understanding and useful feelings have to be translated into prompt action, and healthy discipline is the key in doing this. As we repeatedly act promptly with right motive and appropriate feeling, we establish healthy habits. Besides healthy routines, we can benefit from acting on good opportunities and preventing ourselves from falling prey to temptations. We may hesitate to act or even give up if we feel overwhelmed by a situation. In such cases, it is better to take one day at a time or deal with small parts of the big issue at any one time. Reinforcing our steps by our own and other's encouragement is useful.

CRISIS AND TEMPTATIONS

Crisis is often the opportunity for transformation. We usually change because we see the light--a vision for a better life--or feel the heat of suffering caused by our old patterns. Some hog-farmers, for example, say that the pig looks up only when it is hit on the head. Similarly, many people with personality disorders often won't change without feeling the heat.

The crisis in a beloved person's life can be an opportunity for us to be helpful to alleviate suffering and to promote strength. As an example, when an alcoholic gets into an accident and is hospitalized with injuries, it is quite appropriate for the loving family members to urge the person to seek treatment for the addiction. Those gentle souls who think they should not pressure somebody who is already down are quite mistaken. This is not kicking someone who is down; it is helping the person to use a wonderful opportunity. And if the alcoholic thinks the family members are being unfair, it is only part of the "stinking thinking" of an addict.

Unlike crises, temptations are attractions, desires, or wishes to meet needs in unhealthy ways. We can be very intensely tempted by opportunities to meet passions and addictions, and we need to exercise caution to avoid falling for temptations.

Our good judgment and self-control can be overcome by stimulation of desires for which we have weakness, even if we have strong self-discipline in other matters. Unhealthy habits and addictions are such weak points, and so it is very wise to guard against them. Alcoholics Anonymous recommends "changing playmates and playgrounds," which involves changing friends from drinking buddies to sober ones and places of fun activities from bars to non-drinking situations. Alcoholics who follow this recommendation thereby minimize their exposure to the temptation to drink, but those recovering alcoholics who are overconfident about their self-control and mix with their former drinking buddies invariably relapse.

The strong power of certain temptations may cause the fall of even great individuals. The Bible reveals how King David's passion was aroused intensely after seeing beautiful Bathsheba bathing (which may not have happened had he seen her fully clothed) and led him to commit adultery with her and later cause the death of her husband. Similarly, in a myth in the Hindu epic *Mahabharata*, an ascetic who saw a beautiful woman bathing in the river, lost self-control and had sex with a deer. So, beware of powerful temptations, be it bathing beauties, intoxicants, power trips or others.

Frequently, as temptations get stronger, self-control gets weaker. For instance, in cases of exhibitionism (flashing), a gradual progression of emotional and sexual arousal with exhibitionistic fantasies occurs and finally leads to the act of exhibiting. Exhibitionists have fairly good self-control early on in the chain of events, and teaching them ways to stop at this stage by using better outlets helps. If, however, the chain of events progresses, they increasingly lose self-control. Two respectable professional men were among the people I have treated for exhibitionism; both were conscientious men who worked hard and overcame this condition.

Some people and cultures are too cautious and many others not cautious enough about temptations. Many people think if a particular situation is too tempting for them, it must be so for others also. For instance, several religious groups practice a total ban of alcohol without realizing that a vast majority of adults can enjoy it without harm. On the other hand, many alcoholics unrealistically think they can stop with one or two drinks. One person's healthy pleasure may be another person's addiction.

EXCESSIVE ATTACHMENT TO A NEED

One reason for excessive attachment to a need, even to a particular way of dealing with that need, is using that approach to meet many needs in one's life. Addictions are examples of excessive attachments. Take for example John, a middle-aged workaholic, who grew up in a poor family and was determined to be financially secure. Indeed, he worked hard and succeeded in a franchise business, but he had hardly any social, intellectual, recreational, or spiritual interests. Additionally, he and his wife had a very distant relationship and no sex for years. Although he was rich, he still had financial insecurity. John was excessively attached to work because it dealt with many of his needs, although in quite limited ways. It provided him security, esteem from self and others, meaning, relationships, identity, peace with past and future direction. Also since his feelings, thoughts, and actions were mostly connected with work, they all added to his attachment.

Another reason for excessive attachment is cultural conditioning working through their superegos. Patterns related to certain needs that a culture promotes are taken too seriously by some people who cling to them. Thus, some individuals have habits of taking revenge, using force, trying to keep unrealistic image, and the like. Any habit has its own force and it takes great effort to change strong habits. Pride about one's ways makes it harder to change those ways.

Yet another reason for excessive attachment has to do with one's highly impressionable experiences in the past. For instance, children who received lavish praise or hardly any praise may have too much need for esteem from others. Many men and women whose first spouses cheated may have extreme need for proof of fidelity in their second marriages.

Whatever the reason for excessive attachment, it causes suffering either to the person or to others or both. I have seen many marriages fail because of the excessive need for control on the part of one or the other partner. Excessive control leads to loss of control.

CONSCIENCE AND HUMAN NEEDS

Since conscience works better when our feelings are in control, it is important to reduce our level of temptations and other causes of intense feelings. Healthy ways of thinking help us modify feelings and use them to our best advantage. Every aspect of wisdom helps conscience make well-informed, carefully considered choices while love motivates us to pursue the best possible choices. Conscience interacts with our needs as follows:

1. *Awareness.* Healthy functioning of conscience is promoted by open-minded awareness of needs and opportunities or dangers in meeting them; feelings, thoughts, and information increase the awareness. For psychological and especially for spiritual balance, it is important to be aware of excessive attachment to any need. Then one can see ways to find balance.

2. *Decision.* Conscience judges the pros and cons of our choices and makes right choices in dealing with our needs.

3. *Action.* Living by conscience enhances discipline, courage, and caution in acting on our decisions.

4. *Reassessment.* Conscience judges whether our action to meet our needs was useful and fair, based on the results.

Conscience guides and promotes healthy ways of dealing with our needs with wisdom and love. Bede Griffiths, a Catholic monk, great religious scholar, and a student and lifelong friend of C. S. Lewis, observes that human wisdom and love are manifestations of the Divine--the eternal Wisdom and Love.[27] Thus, handling one's needs in tune with one's conscience is living in harmony with the Divine.

5. ELEVATE YOUR ESTEEM

"Man is not free to choose between having or not having 'ideals,' but he is free to choose between different kinds of ideals, between being devoted to the worship of power and destruction and being devoted to reason and love."[28]

Erich Fromm

"**Y**ou have saved my life. I would have killed myself and probably others if you hadn't helped me. I was really on the road to hell with my drinking, drugging, running around, and my temper. I grew up in that sort of thing and I was proud of it. You really changed my mind and showed me what is right. Looking back I can tell you I had a lot of excitements and a bunch of troubles with all that stuff but I was not happy. My wife had stood by me through so much trouble, and now she and I are both happy." This was the gist of Dennis' evaluation of his transformation.

His father was an alcoholic who verbally and physically abused his family and got into fights with others. Dennis believed in the macho ideals of man's superiority over women, use of force and violence to get his way, proving his manliness by seducing and using women, gaining money and power by hook or crook, and using alcohol or drugs for comfort and pleasure. He considered himself a Christian since in his teens he had accepted Jesus as his personal savior and felt safe that he wouldn't go to hell, but he did not pursue his spirituality any further. What pressured him to seek help was a crisis--depression and anxiety caused by financial and marital problems and physical complications from his substance abuse.

Soon after admission to the hospital, he began power struggles with me and the staff. Along with giving medicines for his anxiety and depression, I tried to understand and explain to him the macho values by which he had been living and how he could change and find genuine fulfillment of his needs by using his conscience to guide him. Although he was resistant at first, he opened his mind gradually and made these changes. His wife and good friends reinforced these changes, and he has continued to maintain his progress.

In short, we are endowed with the capacity and the need to judge our choices and our character. Further, we utilize our values in making our choices and in judging ourselves and others. Esteem and values are not luxuries we can ignore but essential needs in fulfilling our hearts and souls.

ESTEEM

As individuals, we need self-esteem which depends on how we measure up when we judge ourselves using our values of good and bad. And, as members of society, we need esteem from others; that is, we want others to think well of us.

Self-esteem is extremely important because our inner peace and happiness depend on it to a great extent. If we measure up to our values, we experience good self-esteem. Conversely, if we violate or fall short of our values, we feel guilt or shame, which lowers self-esteem.

How other people judge us, or the esteem from others, affects our standing in society as well as our self-esteem. Good social standing is particularly important for public figures. Also one has to be extremely careful in going against the strict rules of one's community if that community is likely to use severe punishments. For instance, in some communities in the world, families would even kill women (so called "honor killing") who get romantically involved with men of their choice instead of letting their families arrange their marriages.

How much a person's self-esteem is affected by the opinions of others depends on how much importance the person gives to other people's opinions. If we base our self-esteem on the judgment of others, we give too much power to others; then they can pull our self-esteem up or down like a yo-yo.

Other people's judgment of us can be used as part of the input into our conscience in judging ourselves. We can give due consideration to any useful information or observation from others. We can also recognize the limitation in other people's judgment. While we judge ourselves on the basis of both our action and our intentions, other people judge us on the basis of our actions that they know about and their interpretation of our intentions. Other people's judgment of us may be incorrect because they don't have all the information about our actions and intentions. Therefore, we must take what others say about us with a broad perspective; we must take what is realistic and useful and discard the rest. If we don't take useful feedback from others, we lose a valuable resource.

Flattery is pleasing but it is harmful if we accept it at face value since it would promote false pride in us. Criticism that is constructive and based on realistic, fair judgment increases our awareness about ourselves and motivates us to improve. On the other hand, destructive criticism is like having dirt thrown at us. We can try to duck the dirt, and if some of the mud hits us, we can clean it off and not rub it in. Too often I notice people rubbing in the dirt thrown at them, that is, taking destructive criticism to heart resulting in unhealthy guilt and shame.

Guilt comes from going against our values and performing undesirable actions; shame can come both from doing things that fall short of our values and from our sense of inferiority in who we are--our identity. Many obese women, for instance, feel guilty about overeating and ashamed of their identity as fat "slobs." Low social or job status can also evoke shame about identity.

In any case, guilt and shame can be healthy or unhealthy. Healthy guilt and shame alert us to actions or intentions that are against our ideals and motivate us to change for the better. Unhealthy guilt and shame, on the contrary, cause us to wallow in negative feelings, lower our self-esteem, and keep us unhappy.

The nine R's of healthy guilt/shame and the contrasting features of unhealthy guilt/shame are:

HEALTHY GUILT/SHAME	UNHEALTHY GUILT/SHAME
Recognizes the real wrongdoing (realistic perception) and the situation, motivation, and consequences of the action	Perception is distorted (based on fleeting thoughts, or someone else's faults or one's own faults exaggerated)
Regrets the wrongdoing in proportion to the seriousness of the action; feels angry, sad, and bad to a realistic extent; has some anxiety and sadness	Regrets intensely based on distorted perception; feels angry, sad, and bad excessively; has significant anxiety and sadness
Repairs damage caused by the wrongdoing in loving, caring ways such as confessing, asking forgiveness, and making amends	Instead of repairing damage, energy is wasted on negative feelings, depression, and anxiety and becomes withdrawn or angry or abusive
Repetition of wrongdoing prevented by understanding underlying causes and circumstances and making positive changes	Use excessive guilt/shame, fear, and punishment of self to prevent repetition; underlying causes may not be understood and corrected
Resolution of negative feelings after useful actions to repair damage and prevent repetition are taken; confessing to a helpful person enhances this process	Continuation of negative feelings and unhealthy reactions whenever memory of the wrongdoing comes up; no acts of confession or confessing to a person who aggravates negative feelings
Rejoicing in the positive changes in oneself	Continuation of negative feelings and self-punishment
Remembers the wrongdoing for healthy purpose of prevention of similar deeds in future; this memory enhances wisdom	Remembers past wrongdoing and hates and punishes oneself; negative attitude and behavior spoil relationships

Rejuvenation of goodness enhances spiritual and psychological strength	Continuing negative feelings harm spiritual and psychological strength
Results in positive self-image and compassion	Results in negative self-image and judgmentalism

In general, the parable of the prodigal son in the Bible (Luke 15: 11-32) illustrates the workings of healthy and unhealthy guilt. The prodigal son got his share of his inheritance, wasted it on worldly adventures, and ended up broken and miserable enough to eat pigs' slop. He finally recognized his mistake, felt guilty, and repaired his wrongdoing by returning to his father and asking for forgiveness. The father welcomed the prodigal son and celebrated his transformation, but the prodigal's older brother resented the warm welcome and homecoming celebration for his brother, probably because the older brother did not share his father's love and wisdom.

Unhealthy guilt/shame causes people to act like the older brother, hold on to negative feelings about the past, fail to enjoy tranquillity and celebration at the present, and prevent a better future resulting from reconciliation and love. Healthy guilt/shame permits people to act like the remorseful son who returned to a healthy relationship, and his loving and wise father who accepted and celebrated the change. The celebration of transformation is very useful, for it affirms reconciliation, enhances self-esteem, and reinforces goodness. Such positive resolution of guilt/shame cuts off the negative pull from the past, provides peace at the present, and promotes better future.

As I said in chapter one, *what is healthy is a therapeutic dose of guilt, neither an overdose of guilt nor lack of guilt, and the same is true for shame.* One of my patients who suffered from excessive guilt about some things and not enough guilt from other things found it useful to put a sign on her refrigerator: *Use therapeutic dose of guilt.* Healthy operation of conscience produces realistic guilt/shame. A rigid superego produces unhealthy or excessive guilt/shame, and a loose superego does not produce enough realistic guilt/shame.

Besides unhealthy guilt/shame, not taking due credit causes low self-esteem. Many individuals do not give themselves accurate, sufficient feedback for doing or being good. Some people are afraid it is selfish or wrong to give oneself good strokes, while others are afraid they will become too proud if they acknowledge their own good deeds.

In such a case, Jane, who was in her forties, suffered from depression and anxiety. Even though she had a stressful, managerial job in a fairly big company, she functioned well at work and helped family members as well as many indigent children. However, Jane felt it would be selfish and improper for her to take credit for her altruistic actions. On the other hand, she felt unreasonable guilt for every little mistake she made and for things that went wrong around her because of somebody else's fault.

Jane had learned to feel unhealthy guilt/shame from two sources. First, her mother had given the distorted impression that Jane was selfish. Secondly, a version of Christian teachings gave Jane the impression that it would be selfish and sinful to feel good about good deeds. She was afraid that she might become conceited by taking credit for her goodness. Exploring these issues clarified Jane's confusion and enabled her to take the credit she deserved and have good self-esteem as well as healthy humility.

WAYS TO PROMOTE SELF-ESTEEM

- Become aware of what your real values are. Know what makes you feel good or proud and what makes you feel ashamed or guilty. Clarify your values. Determine whether your feelings are giving you correct signals and whether or not your values are healthy or need modification.
- Live by spiritual values, do spiritual exercises, and have spiritual identity.
- Let the loving and fair guidance of conscience be a deep source of positive feelings. If you do wrong, experience the

realistic guilt from your conscience, repair the damage you caused, take steps to prevent repetition, and feel good again.

- Become aware of all the good things about yourself such as skills, knowledge, achievements of various sorts, and personal qualities including compassion, honesty, dedication to work, and family. Feel good about these.
- Build on your strengths.
- Develop positive, mutually beneficial relationships.
- Reinforce good feelings, positive thoughts, and constructive actions.
- Prevent your dislikes or disapproval of some aspects about yourself from spreading to other aspects.
- Accept compliments for what they are really worth.
- Let go of any unrealistic fear of being conceited. Unless you tend to be arrogant, the fear of becoming conceited is unrealistic. If this fear is a concern, put it in perspective. Then gradually face the fear, reinforce each step, and overcome the fear.
- Recognize the fiction behind advertisements that make you feel as if you have to buy some products to feel worthy.
- Let unrealistic expectations and ideals go.
- Accept realistic limits, including the fact that hard work does not guarantee achievement of a goal.
- Have relationships with people who have healthy values and who give you good feedback.
- Join support groups if you are dealing with specific psychological problems.
- Learn to block out, ignore, and neutralize in your own mind the destructive criticisms of others.
- Prevent other peoples' prejudices and stereotypes from affecting you; focus on good ideas.
- Determine who your heroes and heroines are and why. It is useful to have people of conscience as heroes and heroines.
- Become aware of, focus on, and expand aspects of your life that are consistent with your ideals. Shift your attention away from those aspects of yourself that you dislike to ones you like. If you have to live with some aspect of yourself that you

dislike, follow the advice I have heard attributed to Mark Twain—"if you have to swallow a frog don't look at it too long." Thus, you may have to shut your eyes, hold your nose, and swallow some unpalatable realities.

VALUES

Our own and other people's judgments are based on the values or ideals as to what is right and wrong or good and bad. Different groups within a nation or community have their own values. Often, many groups have a mixture of spiritual and materialistic/hedonistic values.

1. *Spiritual Values.* Spiritual values are guided by the spirit of the Golden Rule, the ethical principles of nurturing and not harming oneself, and a sense of moral consequence to our actions. This guidance includes a sense of responsibility and respect for the rights of others and oneself. Further, it goes beyond the requirements of the laws and the cultural norms; indeed, living by spiritual values involves abiding by the dictates of a well-informed conscience.

Spiritual values emphasize the *spirit* of rules and regulations. Thus Rabbi Hillel, who accepted a challenge to stand on one leg and recite the whole Torah, stood on one leg and summed up all the laws of the Torah in the principle that we must not do to others what we would not want them to do to us. Jesus summarized the Ten Commandments into the two principles of love of God and love of others as we love ourselves. The Buddha taught the "Four Reliances": Rely on the teacher's message, not on the teacher's personality; rely on the meaning of the teaching, not just on the words of the teacher; rely on the deeper meaning, not on the provisional meaning; rely on one's wisdom mind, not on one's judgmental mind.

Application of such deeper principles helps us use our consciences rather than mechanically follow some rules and find loopholes for selfish purposes. Although social and religious rules have to be taken seriously, the basic principles of values deserve our utmost allegiance.

Spiritual values give much importance to our motive. Doing the right thing is important, but doing it for the right reason is also essential. Truth, goodness, discipline, and wisdom are given high priority in the spiritual value system. Genuine effort with good intention--the spiritually healthy process, not the final outcome of an act--is the key to spiritual living. The outcome is also significant as it helps us reassess our action and enhance our awareness, thus enriching our wisdom and modifying our future choices.

Whereas only one of the AA's twelve steps is about belief in a Higher Power, seven steps are about ethical living--taking moral inventory, confessing wrongs, being ready for and asking God to remove one's character defects, making a list to make amends and acting on it, and taking moral inventory regularly. I find it extremely useful for addicts to use these steps with the understanding and guidance of conscience.

Most religious groups proclaim their brands of morality, but there are many common values. At the Second Parliament of World Religions held in Chicago in 1993--one hundred years after the First Parliament--a crucial event was the declaration of a global ethic that spoke out against religious fanaticism and emphasized the Golden Rule. It called for a commitment to nonviolence, economic and social justice, tolerance, truthfulness, partnership between men and women, and protection of the environment. It taught against sexual coercion, exploitation and discrimination, and false propaganda.

Morality has been found to be the most important characteristic of the resilient people growing up in dysfunctional families but become strong and happy individuals. Far from internalizing the values and examples of their mean or criminal parents, such children use their own consciences and keep their inner goodness, take responsibility, and fight the wrongs in their environment. In my experience, resilient children also find and connect with good people. One of my patients grew up in a terribly dysfunctional (physically, emotionally, and sexually abusive) home with several siblings. A caring and good lady in the neighborhood took an interest in these children, but only my patient made use of her goodness--her siblings did not utilize the opportunity. The close contacts with this neighbor for several years helped my patient be stronger than her siblings. Although she herself had problems with depression, they were minor compared to the severe personality disorders and depressions her siblings suffered.

Spiritual values accept the importance of material well-being and pleasure when it is in harmony with conscience. Materialistic/hedonistic values, however, evade or contradict conscience.

2. *Materialistic/Hedonistic Values.* The materialistic ideal is basically that the more possessions, power, and prestige one has, the better; also, it doesn't matter how these are gained as long as it is legal. Moreover, being fair and responsible to others is not important at all if one can avoid overall material losses. Materialistic people identify closely with their possessions and positions of power, and are shallow. They do not use their consciences much, if at all, and they feel good when they gain power and positions. For example, members of gangs who believe in intimidation and violence rate themselves high as they commit such wrongs. Religious cult members also may gain strong self-esteem and esteem of their colleagues by blindly obeying the cult's leader and fanatically following the cult's ideology.

Hedonistic values are similar to materialistic values except that here pleasure is the most important ideal. Often people live by materialistic/ hedonistic values [to simplify matters, from here on when I use the term materialistic, I include hedonistic also] of the four P's--possessions, power, prestige, and pleasure--which suit our social animal parts at the expense of our spiritual parts. This conflict of values causes much confusion in society.

CONFUSION OF VALUES IN SOCIETY

People are often confused about spiritual and materialistic values. For example, some people who *live* by spiritual values and deserve good self-esteem *judge* themselves by materialistic values and have low self-esteem.

The frequent bombardment by materialistic values makes it difficult for us to judge by spiritual values.

Linda Tschirhart Sanford and Mary Ellen Donovan have identified a syndrome they call "I'm a good woman, so what?" in reference to good women who have low self-esteem. These women look down on themselves "because kindness, caring, nurturing, and other qualities associated with being a good woman are not highly valued in our culture."[29] It is not only women but also men who face low self-esteem despite being good people, if they fail by materialistic values.

An interesting example of a good person with poor self-esteem is a man I once treated for depression. He was very hardworking, honest, and lived by spiritual values. His company pressured him to work excessively, and gradually he became unable to maintain the workload. His employer was not understanding as my patient suffered burn out; finally, he lost his job. Judging himself harshly as a worthless person, he became severely depressed.

Although antidepressants eased most of his depressive symptoms, he continued to judge himself very critically and remained suicidal. So, I confronted him dramatically in an attempt to change his attitude. I questioned whether he was truly spiritual or just a hypocrite who said he believed in spirituality. I wondered aloud why he would not judge himself by spiritual rather than by materialistic values if he really were a spiritual person. When I pushed him hard on this issue, he became quite anxious for a short while. He fumbled, was silent for some time, thought deeply, and then spoke with much excitement. "Doctor, you have opened my eyes. I see what I was doing. I lived right, played by the rules, and worked hard. I was very loyal to my family and my employer. What happened to me is like an accident; it was beyond my control. I have been judging myself wrongly. I have reasons to feel good about myself if I judge myself correctly." Later he told the nurses that he just had a great spiritual awakening which helped to improve his self-esteem and clear his suicidal thoughts.

As in the above case, the values associated with money cause confusion and conflict for many spiritual people who live in highly materialistic cultures. The Bible teaches that "the love of money is the root of all evil" (1 Timothy 6:10), and Jesus emphasized the impossibility of serving two masters—-God and Mammon (Matthew 6:24). Because money is connected with our various needs, it is really important in our lives. So, we cannot ignore it, but we can use our consciences in deciding how we make, keep, and spend money.

Many opposing values are preached and practiced by various people in our society. Some believe in earning money by hard work; others believe in making a fast buck by clever schemes or even illegal scams. Gambling is encouraged by many and discouraged by many others. Honesty is said to be "the best policy", but half-truths, spins, defensible lies, and plain bullshit are common and even respected by many if it suits their agenda. Tooting one's own horn is considered shameful by some but smart salesmanship by others. Sobriety is hailed or ridiculed, and intoxication is admired as adventure or admonished as foolhardiness.

Confusion about moral relativism is widespread, and people who argue that morality is totally relative to a particular culture take this view to an extreme. Of course, there are cultural variations in morality, but the common ethical principles to live by are far more important. The fact that members of 125 different religious groups from various parts of the world--representatives from all the world religions--adopted a basic global ethic at The Second Parliament of World's Religions shows there is common ground in values. The global ethics is consistent with conscience.

The issue of moral relativism is similar to the issue of food and nutrition. With all the different types of food and methods of preparation, there are common components that are healthy and others that are unhealthy. And even the healthy components become unhealthy when taken to extremes.

Morality is not always a clear-cut set of rules, and there are circumstances when breaking the rules may be a reasonable choice. In *Les Miserables* the bishop, a man of conscience, misled the police to protect Jean and transform his life. The people who rescued Jews from

Hitler had to lie and cheat the Nazis. Such exceptions are *not* excuses for undermining valid rules.

Moreover, our ideals are not only about the ultimate issues of life but also about numerous everyday aspects of our lives including etiquette. The original meaning of "etiquette" in French was the label on a package indicating what is inside; today the word means expected behavior that is socially appropriate in various situations. We often pick up ideals from peers, friends, and religious and other social groups, and from the mass media. Many spiritual and mental health groups rightly point out that the extreme level of violence and sexual affairs shown on television has an unhealthy influence on people, especially youngsters.

Many values are really matters of taste rather than something of deep significance, and many daily frustrations, irritations, anger, and even quiet desperation are due to conflicts over minor matters, not life or death issues. Therefore, it is very helpful to distinguish major from minor values, and stand firm in matters that really matter and be flexible in matters that are unimportant in the larger scheme of life.

Sometimes people give too much importance to an action because of its symbolic meaning. For example, when a spouse snores, some couples are pragmatic and sleep in separate rooms without letting the separation lower their love or sexual satisfaction. In fact, these couples have a more intimate and loving relationship than couples who cannot accept the idea of sleeping separately because one of the spouses thinks it symbolizes an unhappy marriage. Couples who use their consciences choose what is beneficial over what seems symbolically important or what merely looks good.

Undoubtedly, we have become more flexible about dress codes, hairstyles, conversational manners, and the like in recent times. This is psychologically and spiritually fine so long as no harm is done. In fact, it is wonderful that we do not have to get bogged down with unimportant demands of superego on such matters. But there are people who are stuck with overgrown superego. For example, an older gentleman refused to allow an excellent young surgeon to treat him because the surgeon wore his hair long. For the older man, the long hair was indeed a hair-raising issue. Some people apply the slippery slope argument or the domino theory excessively. For them any deviation from old traditions is the beginning of the domino effect that would end up in ultimate disaster; this is unhealthy rigidity.

IDEALS WE LIVE BY VERSUS WHAT WE PROFESS

Our true endearing ideals are what we live by and struggle to follow, not the ones we talk about or use as an impressive mask to hide the real picture. However, somebody may be genuinely struggling to reach an ideal he or she professes. In that case the person is not a hypocrite.

Some individuals quit attending church because they mistakenly think they are hypocrites since they are not yet living according to the ideals of the church, although they are trying hard to live up to those ideals. They are not hypocrites so long as they genuinely believe in and are trying to live according to the ideals of the church. In fact, I encourage such people to keep up their church activities because participation can help them in their struggle to improve. Similarly, some alcoholics quit going to AA because they are not completely sober yet and consider it hypocrisy to keep up with AA while they are still drinking. In such cases the person needs to realize that spiritual values emphasize the attempts to do better, not just the final product of doing well. Those who are truly trying to transform their lives for the better deserve their own and other people's appreciation for their effort.

Of course, it would be hypocrisy if someone were involved in religious or spiritual activities, self-help groups, or in professional therapy only to impress others. That is hypocrisy, which goes against conscience.

Expressing good ideas and ideals is useful for us and others if we are genuine. It helps to reinforce our convictions and encourage similar ideas in others. Obviously, talk can be cheap and ultimately more harmful if it is done mostly to impress the listener. Such talking games sadly discourage psychological and spiritual health. Unfortunately, market-oriented societies tend to foster the talking game as a part of the ability to sell.

One of the major confusions of our times is between the market-value of something and its real worth, significance, or usefulness. According to the often quoted view of Oscar Wilde, a cynic knows the price of everything but not the value of anything. Cynicism and the widespread materialistic values are confusing vast numbers of people. For example, a really good book may not become popular because of lack of publicity or other market factors. That does not mean that the ideas in the book are less worthwhile than a book that has sold far more copies because of sensationalism.

There is an unfortunate trend in the mass media to give more importance to controversy than to what is significant and useful for people. Charismatic and slick personalities in particular are capable of creating false impressions and selling goods or ideas that are really not worthwhile. A person with spiritual value would go beyond the market values and look for the real worth.

LEGALISM AND LITIGIOUSNESS

A common form of extremism in our society is litigiousness and legalism. When Becky was going through a divorce from her affluent husband, she told me, "My attorney told me about many ways we could really take my husband to the cleaners. I told her that I want to be fair to my husband although I am mad at him." Becky's conscience guided her to be fair. Had she chosen to exploit her husband, she would have dirtied her own conscience and become more depressed than she already was. When people "take others to the cleaners," in essence they are soiling their own souls.

Law and order are very important for any civilized society; however, excessive use of law, literal application of rules disregarding their good purpose, and the selfish, unfair, exploitative, and destructive use of legal means damage individuals and societies. Just as truth is said to be the biggest casualty of war, conscience and genuine spirituality are victims of legalism and litigiousness.

Numerous Christians who staunchly support St. Paul's teachings against sexual immoralities (1 Corinthians Chapter 6) ignore his condemnation of Christians suing each other in the beginning of the same chapter. In many cases I have seen couples going through divorce, heirs handling inheritance, and people who want to exploit or revenge others taking legal means without using their consciences. Many peoples' superegos support such a stance because of their social conditioning.

On television and in other situations we can notice people using legalistic angles of arguments to support their selfish and superficial stance instead of seeing the broad picture. Extremists from two sides arguing based on their narrow angles give a distorted picture rather than a balanced perspective. The excluded middle ground is often the more relevant and useful part of the issue.

Legalism in religions goes with rigid superego rather than conscience. Jesus' assertion that Sabbath is made for man and not the other way around, indicates rejection of a legalistic approach. Healthy spirituality transcends legalism.

HUMILITY AND ESTEEM

Along with self-esteem, humility has an important place in fulfilling our hearts and souls. All the great world religions consider humility a virtue. Many people describe humility, awe before the tremendous mystery of the Divine, as part of their religious experience. Humility comes from the word "humus" or earth. By our humility, we stay in touch with our earthliness and do not have our heads in the clouds or our noses up in the air. Humility is not low self-esteem; in fact, it accompanies good self-esteem. If we judge by our consciences, we would notice our limitations, weaknesses, and shortcomings and have healthy humility.

There are several benefits from humility: openness to learn, willingness to seek help because of the awareness of limitations and weaknesses, depth of perception, and being compassionate and loving.

An interesting story talks about a professor who visited a humble Zen master in the master's hut. After some discussion, it was time for tea. As the professor held his cup, the master kept pouring tea, even after the cup was full. The tea spilled over onto the floor. This was quite puzzling to the professor. Then the master explained that he could not help the professor until the professor's mind had room to receive the knowledge. When we are "full of it," we lack humility and openness to change.

One of the major reasons for avoidance of depth and truth is our fear of hurting our pride. Humility overcomes such fears. Philosopher Nietzsche once stated that his memory said that he did something wrong, but his pride said he did not and his pride won. Humility can prevent such self-deception. Many of the self-defeating games we play (as we saw in Chapter Three) are to protect our esteem.

The "male ego" often prevents men from admitting their problems, especially emotional and spiritual problems, and seeking help. In protecting their own false pride, such men tend to look down on those who seek therapy. Also, humble people are more compassionate and nurturing to themselves and others than people with false pride.

Socrates rightly observed that wisdom begins with the admission of our ignorance. With humility and honesty as we examine life, we can grow in wisdom. And as we live by and judge by well-informed consciences, we will have strong self-esteem and healthy humility, which can contribute greatly to our fulfillment.

6. KEEP A HEALTHY IDENTITY

> "Never, never, even in their moments of richest and wildest happiness, were they unaware of a sublime joy in the total design of the universe, a feeling that they themselves were a part of the whole, an element in the beauty of the cosmos. This unity with the whole was the breath of life to them."[30]
>
> Boris Pasternak

Identity, our sense of who we are, has two aspects: *individuality* or uniqueness and *group identity* or having unity with others. Both aspects of identity, being apart from others and being a part of others, play a significant role in fulfilling our hearts and souls.

INDIVIDUALITY

The word "individual" comes from the Latin root *"individuus,"* which means indivisible. Each person's unique body and body image, personality, ideas, ideals, beliefs, age, gender, occupation, possessions, position, roots, and shoots (future projection)etc. combine to form his or her indivisible whole, his or her distinct, individual identity.

A dramatic experience some years ago clearly showed me the importance of having one's own identity, a sense of separateness from others. I was treating Tony, a young man with schizophrenia. He was almost mute, did not eat regularly, never smiled, and would not shake hands. With a smile on his face one morning, he shook hands with me and said, "Now I know that you are you and I am me." He explained that for a few weeks he did not know where he ended and others began, and sometimes he did not eat because when somebody else ate, he felt that he was eating. As he progressed, he had regained his sense of individuality.

Body image, an important element of our individuality, includes a sense of body size, shape, gender, skin, hair color, musculature, and strength. How we feel about our body image often depends on how our body compares to the "ideal" body presented by advertisements and the mass media. Currently in the United States, the ideal male is strong and muscular, while the ideal female is slim with large breasts. Since few individuals have "ideal" bodies, many people dislike their body image.

A sense of our intelligence, knowledge, skills, likes and dislikes, ideas and ideals also provides us with vital information as to who we are. Accurate self-awareness of individual characteristics helps us decide which features to nurture or restrict and what social roles/careers are most suitable for us. For example, an introverted person would find sales jobs particularly frustrating.

A distorted perception of our individuality can cause psychological and spiritual problems. For instance, Linda was slim but thought for many years that she was obese and wasted a great deal of energy, time, and money trying to stay slim. She gave extremely high priority to her distorted body image. Her husband and family found her too self-absorbed and stubborn. She did not develop much of her intellectual, aesthetic, and spiritual potential because she was so preoccupied with her physical appearance. With therapeutic help and great struggles, Linda achieved a more balanced and broader identity and thus a better life-style.

A body image survey by *Psychology Today*[31] magazine found that psychological and social well-being was not related to the importance people gave to appearance. Those who focused on health and fitness rather than body image had positive feelings about their appearance. It is best to keep first things first; that is, keep health and fitness, not body image, first. Conversely, surveys by *Psychology Today* in 1972, 1985, and 1997 showed increasing dissatisfaction with body image-- twenty-five, thirty-eight, and fifty-six percent of women and fifteen, thirty-four, and forty-three percent of men were dissatisfied with their overall appearance.[32]

In my experience with women who had undergone removal of one or both breasts, the spiritually oriented women handled the change of body image far better than other women. The women who had given excessive importance to being sexy and associated it with big breasts had the hardest time accepting the change.

We can celebrate the advances in plastic surgery, especially in correcting deformities, and recognize the benefits many people derive from cosmetic surgery. At the same time, people can have good identity and self-esteem by accepting body images that differ from popular models.

Our values form another important part of our identity both in our uniqueness and our unity. Some people give so much importance to their values that they are willing to sacrifice a lot, even their own lives, for the sake of their great values. Socrates is admired for this kind of a sacrifice, but extremists who have superficial values and narrow identity are not admirable.

INDIVIDUALITY AND RELATIONSHIPS

Individuality is damaged to varying degrees by either excessive attachment to oneself as in individualism or egocentrism, or to others as in dependent and codependent relationships. If we apply Aristotle's idea that virtue is the golden mean between the extremes--and the extremes are vices--authentic individuality is the virtue; egocentrism and dependency/codependency are vices.

EGOCENTRISM

Authentic (true to one's deepest self) individuality is quite different from excessive individualism or egocentrism, a difference that is significant because many societies promote egocentrism in the name of individuality. Egocentrism, which takes the individual aspect of identity too far, shortchanges the relationship part of identity and creates an imbalance.

Authentic individuals have deep and balanced identity, giving the proper place to the personal, social, and spiritual elements. On the other hand, egocentrists tend to give excessive importance to their superficial personal aspects at the expense of the social and spiritual elements of life. They may have many superficial connections, even tight ones, but not deep relationships.

Some egocentrists are contrarians. They voice opinions that are contrary to other people's, not because of genuinely different insight but to show their uniqueness. Such people are difficult to communicate with, unlike authentic individuals who are a delight to dialogue with, whether one agrees or disagrees with them. Furthermore, authentic people respect the authenticity of others. They appreciate depth, openness, and integrity, and share from the depth of their being without attempting to manipulate.

HOW TO DEVELOP AUTHENTIC INDIVIDUALITY

- Use your conscience.
- Increase awareness of your individual tendencies, skills, wishes, visions, likes, and dislikes.
- Reinforce your positive qualities.
- Change negative qualities, if possible, and accept what cannot be changed.
- Develop your own reasoning and intuition.
- Practice solitude. The practice of meditation is very useful in promoting solitude and one's overall individuality.
- Be willing to express your ideas, wishes, etc.
- Also be willing to negotiate and make compromises.
- Recognize your defenses and let go of excesses.
- Give productive expression to your powers.
- Give up egocentric tendencies.
- Develop habits of reading and reflecting.
- Increase your knowledge about significant matters.
- Pursue artistic interests.
- Follow the example of authentic individuals.

DEPENDENCY AND CODEPENDENCY

Dependency and codependency involve being too attached to someone else. Once within a couple of weeks, I had two female patients who told me they were codependent according to what they learned by reading. Neither woman worked outside the home or had children to care for, nor were they emotionally, sexually, or in other ways very giving to their husbands. The husbands worked hard and were frustrated by not getting their intimacy needs met; they showed affection but were not as emotionally supportive as the wives wanted them to be. Both women were too dependent and had not actualized much of their own potentials. They took a lot from their spouses and gave very little in return but still complained because they wanted even more. They talked about the possibility of divorce, even though they realized they couldn't financially or emotionally afford it.

The basic difference between dependents and codependents is that dependents take too much or lean too heavily on others and codependents give too much or let others lean heavily on them in their close relationships. Both types may have low self-esteem, frustration, anger, excessive need for control, weak boundaries in their close relationships, sexual problems, difficulty in trusting, and repression. Usually, codependents work and socialize far better than dependents. In fact, codependents may be strong individuals with one big weakness in close relationships; they give too much in a relationship that provides very little in return. When I told some women that they were not codependents but dependents, they disliked it at first. After all, codependency is more socially acceptable. But as they learned more about their dependence and how they could become authentic persons with interdependent relationships, they were willing to try it.

Dependent and codependent people act like the extension of somebody else; they are nobody unless they are part of somebody else. Dependent people may or may not be selfish. The unselfish dependents lean on others heavily because they did not develop their own abilities to function authentically, and they give what they can in their relationships. Codependents give excessively in the hope of fulfilling their own needs for identity and intimacy. A codependent woman worked hard and took care of her alcoholic husband who did not keep a steady job and abused her off and on until she got therapy and broke off the relationship.

Dependents and codependents often show strict superego and their self-esteems depend heavily on the opinion of people to whom they are attached. They benefit tremendously when they learn to use their consciences well instead of following their harsh superegos and taking others' opinions too seriously.

One dependent young female I treated acted like her husband's tail; she had no firm opinions, ideas, wishes, hopes, or dreams about life apart from those of her husband. Her husband enjoyed dominating her early on, but he got bored with her after many years. Even in simple matters such as choosing a restaurant she would answer by guessing what his preference might be, ignoring her own wishes. She came from an authoritarian family and religious background, but stifling her individuality did not really make her happy. So she was willing to reexamine her pattern. Fortunately, her husband was going through a crisis that opened his mind to change from an authoritarian to a genuinely loving relationship. With his changes and the insight and support from therapy, she developed her authentic individuality.

Dependents not only lean too heavily on others, but they also often lean on partners who exploit or abuse them. While a dysfunctional family background may initiate dependency and codependency, these people often perpetuate their problems by the type of partners they choose.

The very aptly named Echo in Greek mythology is a classic dependent. She has no voice of her own, but echoes other people's voices. Unfortunately, she falls in love with Narcissus, a handsome young man who could love only himself. Deeply dejected by Narcicuss' rejection, Echo dies. Narcissus, an egocentrist, later dies too in a deadly embrace of his own reflection in water. Such are the tragedies of dependency and egocentrism.

The following table contrasts authentic individuality with egocentrism and dependency:

EGOCENTRISM	AUTHENTIC INDIVIDUALITY	DEPENDENCY CODEPENDENCY
Sense of individual separateness is too strong	Balanced sense of separateness and belonging	Weak sense of separateness
Boundary of self is rigid and carefully guarded	Boundary of self is fairly flexible yet firm	Weak boundary; easily fuses with others
High insecurity in sharing identity deeply forming a "we" unit	No insecurity in sharing identity deeply; shows healthy caution	Not enough caution in sharing identity
Tends to use others for one's purposes	Neither uses nor lets others use oneself	Tends to be used by others
Tends to be self centered and superficial; superficial in relationships	Has deep relation ship with self, others, and Higher Power	Tends to be superficial; centered on the other
Does not adequately use conscience Unfair to other	Uses conscienc quite well Fair to both	Doesn't use conscience well Unfair to self
Meets needs selfishly	Meets needs lovingly	Meets needs by dependency
Close-minded (rigidly closed)	Open-minded (reasonably open)	Too open (rigidly open)
Proud	Good self-esteem	Low self-esteem
Low humility	Good humility	Excess humility

Pecking Order and Group Identity

Our relationships to others form several pieces of our identity puzzle. Human beings and many animals establish a pecking order or social hierarchy.

Research done at Auburn University on milk-producing cows underscored the importance of social hierarchy. Cows are highly social animals and maintain a well-recognized hierarchy, with some of the cows, usually the bigger ones, dominating. To maximize milk production and feed efficiency, dairy farmers regroup their cows every few weeks, which disturbs the established social hierarchy. For several days after the regrouping, the dominant cows bite, push, and shove to regain their positions of power, which makes the submissive cows nervous, resulting in lower milk production. The researchers found that spraying the cows with a licorice-scented oil prevented them from recognizing each other through smell, minimized the aggressive behavior, and milk production improved.[33] Wouldn't it be great if similar steps could be taken for human identity conflicts?

Many human conflicts are related to identity. In such conflicts, those who live by their conscience try to be fair to all involved. Besides our sense of our position in a particular group, we also have a sense of various groups that we belong to, based on factors such as work, race, religion, ethnicity, gender, marital status, sexual role, nationality, economic class, and age. If we are too attached to any of these aspects of our identity, it causes problems. For example, a macho male used to become abusive toward his friends if they suggested that he was a softy or a wimp.

Identifying with others who have things in common with us, such as race or gender, is natural; but it becomes a problem when one piece of our overall identity expands too much like a cancer and damages the whole. Racism, sexism, religious extremism, classism, and superpatriotism have two destructive features. First, one aspect of identity becomes too important as the center of identity, and, secondly, the person loses perspective.

VARIOUS IDENTITY "ISMS" CAUSE
THE FOLLOWING PROBLEMS

- A sick sense of superiority of oneself and one's in-group (the group one identifies with)
- Tendency to exploit other groups (the outsiders)
- Prejudiced opinions about other groups
- Hostile attitudes toward members of different groups, which may lead to unfair and even violent actions against other groups
- Lack of realistic guilt about unfairness
- Lack of empathy and presence of sadistic enjoyment in the suffering of out-groups
- Superficiality
- Insecurity about one's own identity

OTHER IDENTITY PROBLEMS

Another identity issue comes from people identifying with their illnesses, such as when a person identifies himself or herself by saying, "I am an alcoholic" or "I am a schizophrenic." This identification with illness is helpful on a limited basis, as in the case of treating addicts because the admission of addiction is the foundation on which recovery is built. But in many cases, the label of a chronic condition discourages the person and may lead to giving up the struggle to do one's best. It is far better to do what is beneficial and keep one's broader identity.

A different identity problem occurs when individuals get stuck emotionally instead of moving along in their life cycle, such as moving from adolescence to adulthood or adjusting to retirement. This problem occurs for many people as a mid-life crisis. Instead of going forward with a renewed healthy identity and finding deeper meaning in life, some people regress and act like teenagers. Such people may try to prove youthful vitality by sexual liaisons with much younger members of the opposite sex, driving dangerously, abusing drugs, and other out-of-character behaviors.

Yet another identity problem manifests itself in unresolved grief. While people in normal grief go through denial, anger, bargaining, depression, and acceptance (as Elizabeth Kubler-Ross observed), some people get stuck in anger or depression and do not reach acceptance; they simply cannot accept the changed identity.

For example, I once treated a woman in her forties who had great expectations for her son. She had not gone to college because of her pregnancy, and she had hoped her son would fulfill her dream of higher education, which was an important part of her identity as a person. Contrary to her wish, however, her son decided to settle for a blue-collar job, which meant that her wishful identity as the mother of a well-educated, successful man did not materialize. Anger and depression troubled her until she developed a healthy, balanced identity of her own, accepting the disappointment of her unfulfilled dreams for herself through her son.

Gender roles of men and women are important part of identity. Traditional roles of men and women have loosened but some people tend to hold on to tradition.

Men customarily have been expected to take the initiative sexually and be aggressive in both providing and protecting. Men often neglected the need for affection for themselves and for the women and children in their families. Likewise, many women have had difficulty being assertive and have relied on men for physical protection for themselves and their children. Many women have also relied on men for the discipline of their children. In the old days men were allowed to physically punish their wives. In fact, the phrase "rule of thumb" comes from the English law that allowed men to beat their wives with twigs not wider than their thumb.

In playing the role of the aggressor, men learned to reinforce anger and repress tender feelings. The notion that strong men do not cry stifled normal human expression of sadness by men and lowered the self-esteem of women who expressed their sadness. Also women were conditioned to excessively restrict both awareness and expression of their aggressive and sexual drives. Now that men and women have more freedom, they can enhance their self-awareness, empathy, compassion, and love.

Many of the relative differences between men and women are useful to recognize so that the two sexes can relate more cooperatively and creatively. Men tend to give more importance to the individuality aspect while women tend to emphasize the belonging aspect of identity. Women want to relate closely by expressing their feelings about problems. On the contrary, men tend to take a problem solving or "fixing things" approach or withdraw instead of meeting women's need to share feelings. Symbols of power are very important to men, and symbols of good relationship are highly valued by women. Such generalizations have plenty of exceptions, and these differences can be bridged.

As social and spiritual beings, men and women have so much in common that the differences are relatively small and wonderfully complementary based on spiritual values. Based on materialistic values, the strong may think it is right to exploit the weak. Such exploitation is clearly contrary to conscience, even if some people's superegos approve the behavior.

In recent times men and women have great opportunities to complement their gender differences better and meet each other's needs in cooperative and creative ways. Increased social, economic, and political freedoms have given us more chances to express authentic individuality and a more balanced sense of belonging. But identity problems persist.

GROUP ALLEGIANCE

Allegiance to one's group is natural, and the need for group identity and group pride is common; and it is healthy if it is in tune with one's conscience. Doing whatever our group approves may please our hearts, but it won't fulfill our souls if it goes against our consciences. Group's sanctions do not sanctify wrongs. To be authentic and truly spiritual individuals, we have to resist peer pressure to do wrong and prevent distorted views or unfairly blaming others in favor of our group. Extremist leaders often get support from members with blind loyalty and do wrongs which increase the group's power and pride at the expense of their spirituality.

Societies that allow individuals the freedom of conscience in matters that are crucial to the group deserve special admiration from a spiritual view. The United States' provision for conscientious objectors to be exempted from military service is such a case.

Jesus commanded his followers to give to Caesar what belonged to Caesar and to God what belonged to God (Matthew 22:21). Just as loving parents see both strengths and weaknesses of their children and nurture the good while discouraging the bad, each of us must discern the strengths and weaknesses of our group and try to reinforce the healthy but discourage the unhealthy aspects. Healthy love, not blind infatuation, allows us to uphold our spiritual values in our group affiliations. If extremists accuse us of not being true members because we don't blindly follow the group's agenda, we can explain our genuine reasons and give others a chance to broaden their perspective, although not many may change. Interestingly, when a Christian minister told President Lincoln that God is on the U. S. side, Lincoln pointed out that U. S. should be on God's side.

ROOTS AND SHOOTS

Our roots, or heritage, form an integral part of our identity. Information about our ancestors, their religious, socioeconomic, and other backgrounds helps us understand our unique heritage. Some people want to know their roots from a few previous generations, while others want to follow their roots further. People who are too attached to their roots can become stuck like trees in their traditional identity, which stifles new growth.

In addition to roots, we have "shoots," the future projection of whom we are trying to become. We need to spend a reasonable amount of time speculating, anticipating, planning, and working toward a good future. Spending too much energy speculating about the future, or being preoccupied with past mistakes, is harmful. We need to prepare for the kind of future we want and also be flexible enough to change our plans if necessary.

SPIRITUAL OR UNIVERSAL IDENTITY

Developing a spiritual identity helps to deepen and center our overall identity. Using spiritual values, the sexes and other warring groups can find peace within themselves and with others. Individuals who reject spirituality can use healthy humanistic identity and values to promote harmony within themselves and with others.

The quote from Pasternak at the beginning of this chapter beautifully describes a universal identity. A friend of mine told me that in his youth he and his buddies enjoyed going out into the wide open countryside on moonlit nights and lying down on the ground so they could appreciate the nature around them and the starry skies above, and experience a sense of connection with the universe. What a rich, lovely spiritual exercise. In peak experiences and Near Death Experience, people sense that everything in the universe is interconnected and their sense of individuality is enhanced. For spiritual people, such universal identity has a spiritual dimension, and so, it is spiritual identity.

HUMAN CAPACITY FOR EMPATHY

The Tao master Chuang Tzu and a disciple Hui Tzu were walking by a river one day. Seeing fishes leaping and darting, Chuang Tzu said that the fishes were happy. Hui argued that Chuang could not know that the fishes were happy since he was not a fish. Chuang Tzu countered that Hui could not know whether Chuang knew since Hui was not Chuang. Then Chuang explained that he knew the fishes were happy through his own experience of happiness. Thus, despite differences we can identify with others based on our commonality.

Karen Armstrong has pointed out an exceptionally interesting method used in ancient Greece to stimulate empathy for the enemy.

Athenians were encouraged to watch plays which contained the sufferings of their enemies, the Persians who had devastated Athens just a few years earlier. And the audience was told to weep aloud in empathy for the sufferings of the Persians. Armstrong goes on to say, "… at the end of the *Oresteia,* the vengeful Erinyes were transformed into the Eumenides, the "well-disposed ones," and given a shrine on the Acropolis. We had to learn to feel with people we have hated and harmed: at the end of the *Iliad,* Achilles and Priam wept together."[34]

Like hatred, prejudices distort our views. I notice two kinds of prejudices, and one of them is the prejudice caused by people making judgments, or accepting opinions, without empathic understanding of somebody else who is different. The old prejudices toward minorities are of this type. The second kind of prejudice is the unfounded belief that someone is incapable of empathizing with and understanding members of a different group. For instance, a very empathic white Christian minister told me sadly that some members of a minority group told him he would not understand their problem because he was not one of them. I have had the interesting experience a few times when some drug addicts told me that I could not understand their problem because I am not a recovering addict myself, in spite of the fact that I have successfully treated numerous addicts. Interestingly, I do not recall any severely mentally ill patients showing this type of prejudice. By using our capacity for empathy, we can understand what others are going through. Of course, if we do not use empathy, we can easily misunderstand those who are different from us. Let us use empathy and help others to do the same. By understanding prejudice, we can prevent being prejudiced against prejudice.

We can enhance our empathy with others by listening to them, watching them, and using our imagination to experience what they experience. Knowledge about human needs, motives, and ways of coping increases our empathy tremendously. Reading great literary works and the stories in religious books also opens our eyes to human dilemmas and conflicts, and ways of dealing with them. The deeper our understanding and the sharper our imagination, the stronger our empathy. Studying the lives and ideas of great people can enhance our empathy, but the rigid and narrow views of bigots can damage our empathy. Dogmatic people who view others through their ideologically-colored glasses miss the clear vision of empathic understanding.

CONSCIENCE AND IDENTITY

Authentic individuality is in tune with conscience. Egocentrism, dependency, and codependency go against   conscience to the extent it promotes unfairness to others and or oneself. Excessive allegiance to any group is also against conscience because it involves unfairness to others.

In *Gandhi's Truth*, Erik Erikson observes that Gandhi prevented "pseudo-speciation"--the tendency of human groups to behave like a different species and act unfairly to other groups based on differences in race, religion, nationality and the like. Typically psuedospeciation results from the accumulation of bad conscience, negative identity, and hypocritical moralism; Gandhi prevented this process.[35] Bad conscience is from doing harm to oneself or others, which Gandhi tried hard to prevent. Negative identity results from identifying with our weaknesses; Gandhi encouraged people to identify with their deepest selves and to recognize and control their weaknesses. Hypocritical moralism overlooks our faults and exaggerates others' faults; Gandhi, who was guided by his conscience, showed a fair assessment of the problems of his own people and those of his opponents. Jesus taught us to remove the beam from our own eyes before we take the mote out of other people's eyes (Matthew 7:4-5). Politicians often minimize or deny the faults of their own group while unfairly blaming opponents for various problems.

Using our consciences we can overcome racism, sexism, and other identity "isms" which are often supported by superegos. We can have a balanced sense of belonging to various groups and a reasonable level of loyalty to any group without being unfair to others. Also, guided by conscience, we can have strong authentic individuality rather than being egocentric or codependent/dependent. True individuality gives due importance to the deeper aspects of our lives. Each person is a unique part of the universal web; affirmation of this true identity of oneself is very beneficial in one's fulfillment.

7. RELATE WELL

A great deal of our fulfillment, or lack of it, depends on how we relate to ourselves, others, the world, and God. A character in a play by the French philosopher Jean Paul Sartre makes the famous statement that hell is other people (individuals with severe personality disorders can remind us of an element of truth in this hyperbole). But the great Persian poet Omar Khayyam provides us with the poetic vision of how even the wilderness can be a paradise with just some bread and wine and our beloved singing.

How we relate to ourselves and God or the spiritual realm is particularly important for two reasons. We have more control over these two relationships, and if these relationships are good, they automatically enhance all of our other relationships.

RELATIONSHIP TO OURSELVES

Shakespeare's great advice, "To thine own self be true" is a crucial principle to follow in trying to fulfill our hearts and especially our souls. So, we must guard against our defenses. An alert conscience, spirit of humility, feeling good about authenticity, and awareness of temptations to lie to ourselves can help us greatly to be authentic. Authenticity is reinforced by the inner peace and strength of integrity that go with it.

Our inner voices and internal dialogues are major parts of our relationship to ourselves. Besides the voices of conscience and superego which I have already discussed, we carry on an internal dialogue which also affects our thoughts, feelings, and actions. Although we cannot stop thoughts from coming into our minds, we can learn to entertain useful thoughts and let other thoughts go, and thus have beneficial inner dialogue. Clearly, therefore, awareness of what goes on in our minds is critical.

Being authentic is being responsible and creative in one's relationship to oneself, that is, being the author of oneself by one's choices and being true to one's own deepest self. Authenticity involves being open-minded and living by one's conscience. Often people interchange the words "authentic" and "independent", which is incorrect because one can be independent by doing one's own thing without using one's conscience. I know many independent people, for instance, who are superficial and selfish, not authentic.

Authentic people promote authenticity rather than dependence or blind conformity. An example is the Buddha's advice not to accept his teaching blindly but to analyze and test it and accept what one finds true. It is difficult to be authentic because we are bombarded by falsehoods, temptations, or pressures of varying degrees from society and from ourselves. At the same time, benefits of authenticity far outweigh the problems from it.

We have to love ourselves. If we hate ourselves for some reason, we must examine the reason and take steps to overcome the problem. If we have done wrong or failed and are wallowing in guilt and shame, we need to deal with these feelings realistically as discussed in Chapter Five.

RELATIONSHIP TO GOD

People try to relate to God in various ways including joining a particular religious group and practicing spirituality. Living in tune with a well informed conscience, spiritual beliefs (see details in Chapter Thirteen), and spiritual exercises are ways to relate well to God. Spiritual exercises include prayer, spiritual reading, listening to spiritual talks, meditation, contemplation, centering prayer (see Appendix) practice of goodness, and pilgrimages. Mystical experiences, Near Death Experiences, and miracles are extremely valuable happenings to be cherished if they occur to us. And even when they happen to others, learning about them can strengthen our relationship to God.

In my experience, when people grow spiritually, many keep their earlier religious affiliation but with a broadened perspective while others change their affiliation. I have known many people who grew up in but later rejected religious extremism with its close-mindedness, rigidity, arrogance, superficiality, selfishness, and meanness and pursued healthy personal growth by using their consciences well. Some of them left their former religious traditions and joined religious or spiritual groups that suited their views while others continued their childhood religious affiliation but pursued their own spiritual growth too.

These two approaches worked well in the case of a couple I have known. The husband found many of the teachings and practices of the Christian denomination of his childhood to be inconsistent with his psychological and philosophical knowledge and ethics. Leaving his former church, he joined another Christian denomination with teachings and practices more consistent with his own. His wife also shared his psychological and spiritual growth, but she did not want to break with their former denomination because of her close social ties. She kept her former church affiliation without letting it damage her spirituality by being selective in following the denomination's teachings.

Our relationships to ourselves and to God or the spiritual realm influence how we relate to the world and to others. We are becoming increasingly aware of our responsibility to do our part in protecting the environment and in promoting peace and prosperity in the world.

TWO BASIC ASPECTS OF RELATIONSHIPS

The two basic aspects of all personal relationships are protection and nurturing, both of which can be healthy or unhealthy. *Healthy protection* is sufficient protection in a given situation. For instance, in relationship with reliable friends, defensiveness should be low because there is little reason to defend one's security or self-esteem.

Healthy nurturing allows us to meet our needs, achieve our potential, and strengthen our weak points without going overboard and greedily taking what belongs to others. Healthy nurturing also involves accepting our particular situation in life and having the will to move toward healthy goals. Some people are unwilling to accept their situation and waste energy fighting the facts rather than moving on. They become like a schoolboy who did not like his starting position in a race, so he threw a temper tantrum instead of running and thereby lost his chance of winning. Many of my patients have hated themselves for being obese, smoking, and other reasons; they did not progress until they stopped wasting their energy in self-hate. Being stuck in anger is not healthy; the smart choice is to use the angry energy to push forward.

Unhealthy protection and nurturing are either excessive or insufficient. This may involve self or others or both.

Excessive protection *of self* manifests in one's being too guarded, suspicious, paranoid, angry, or hypersensitive. It also shows rigidity and excessive use of defenses.

Excessive protection of others includes excessive attempts to control their thoughts, feelings, and actions. Religious cults, for example, limit contacts to outsiders.

Insufficient protection of self manifests in blind trust of others, uncritical acceptance of illogical ideas, taking undue risks, and not using reasonable precautions. Too little self-protection often results in becoming involved and staying in destructive relationships.

Insufficient protection of others in our care results in not setting healthy limits and not enforcing important rules. For instance, parents who do not lay and enforce ground rules regarding studies, curfew hours, friends, and other appropriate concerns fail in their responsibility to protect their children.

Excessive nurturing of self manifests itself in greed, power mongering, arrogance, and superficiality, and an inability to care about others deeply.

Excessive nurturing of others includes, putting others on a pedestal they do not deserve, giving too much tender loving care for others while neglecting oneself, and giving others undue power to control or manipulate oneself.

Insufficient nurturing of self occurs when we neglect our own needs and potential. Excessive protection automatically causes insufficient nurturing.

Insufficient nurturing of others may come from selfishness, rigidity, indifference or hate. Circumstances of life also play a role. Many parents cannot give their children the high levels of nurturing that they want to provide because of economic pressures. People who are conditioned to take care of themselves at everybody else's expense sense no reason to nurture others. Addictions and other excessive attachments also takes away from nurturing others. And some people are so defensive it drains their ability to nurture.

HEALTHY CLOSENESS/DISTANCING IN INTERPERSONAL RELATIONSHIPS

The fact that single, separated, divorced, and widowed people are likely to die four years earlier than married people indicates the benefit of close relationships. Healthy distancing is also important. As an old saying warns, "You can't keep from getting soiled if you fight with a skunk."

We can protect ourselves by keeping a healthy distance from people who are destructive to us. People with personality disorders are typically more or less troublesome to others, especially to people close to them. Signs of excessive dependence or independence, rigidity, lack of realistic guilt, tendency to shift blame, superficiality, irresponsibility, unreliability, and especially meanness and slickness should alert us to keep a safe distance in relating to such individuals. We may have to work with or study with them, or be with them in other situations, but we do not have to develop a close relationship with them.

If you are already in a committed relationship with somebody who has a personality disorder, you need to take a tough-love approach. Allowing yourself to be manipulated is unhealthy for you and for your partner with the personality disorder. Know the value system of those close to you by carefully listening to them and objectively observing their actions. Figure out whether they use their conscience or not, who they admire or dislike and why, and what their ideals are. Keep in mind that people with personality disorders often mask their true nature; so if you are considering a close relationship, find out about them from others too. Look for their values and patterns of behavior. People are capable of changing, but people with personality disorders resist change. If you try hard to help a person with personality disorder to transform without good results, then you can pragmatically accept the poor chance of improvement and save yourself more trouble. People who have made healthy transformation deserve credit for it, but be cautious about potential for relapse.

Many of my patients have tragically allowed themselves to enter into unhappy relationships because they overlooked the other person's past. In one case, a young lady was very unpleasantly surprised to find out that her husband had lied to her about his education, job, and possessions. He had claimed to have a good job and great wealth, and she did not check out these things before marrying him because she trusted him. Even though they had been in school together, she did not know what he had been doing for the fifteen years prior to their marriage. He got her into financial troubles, and only when his legal problems hit them in the face did she realize his true nature.

Looking before leaping into a deep relationship often saves much heartache. Healthy love is wide eyed, not blind. Don't assume that somebody is dependable because he or she is a religious leader or holds a high status. Many people, including religious or social leaders, do not live by their consciences and may be highly successful in terms of power, position, and prestige largely because of their manipulativeness and superficiality. The experience of Karen illustrates the point. She was depressed because of her bitter disappointment with a minister. Karen is a very spiritual person, and she had helped this minister a great deal in a joint business. She trusted him but, as time went on, she was shocked by the extent of his selfishness, meanness, and manipulation.

Checking out a person before developing a relationship helps us choose safe distance and appropriate closeness in the relationship. Healthy closeness/distancing plays a key role in developing healthy relationships.

Healthy interpersonal relationships are mutual, not one sided. If you keep giving and your partner does not reciprocate, there is something wrong. At the same time, happy marriages are often not a matter of reciprocating in kind or splitting all chores into half and half. What is important is to help each other's fulfillment.

In a mother-child relationship the child's response may be very limited compared to the amount of maternal care given, but still there is some response if the child is healthy. In a situation where one partner cannot respond—such as someone in a coma—the other partner continues to support and care because of love and responsibility.

DIFFERENT WAYS OF RELATING

In his book *One to One*, psychoanalyst Theodore Rubin presents four basic ways of relating: cooperative, creative, adversarial, and antagonistic. These four modes of relating are not watertight compartments and in any particular relationship we may move from one mode to another from time to time. For example, there are times when a couple is in an adversarial mood, unlike their usual cooperative and creative spirit. Let us explore these four modes in some detail. In describing these four modes, I have taken some ideas from Rubin and added many of my own.

1. *Cooperative relating*. Cooperative relating reflects a spirit of mutuality and sharing. The partners show flexibility and willingness to go the extra mile. Direct communication, openness, and respect prevail,

while manipulation, power-struggle, and especially the use of force, are absent. With no need to play one-upmanship, teamwork invigorates the partners. Even if they have significant differences on some issues, the partners seek common ground and accept the other's individuality.

2. *Creative relating.* In creative relating the partners bring out the best in each other. Each partner is deeply tuned to the potential of the other, and he or she stimulate creative possibilities while inhibiting destructive or harmful ones. This brings both partners great pleasure. They accept the individuality of the other, while sharing common interests, values, and goals. They communicate directly and openly, and even though they may know each other so well they can accurately guess what is on the other's mind, they do not play the guessing game. They express differences of opinion without being defensive or damaging. Each partner helps make the other's life as fulfilling and happy as possible. They also recognize and accept limitations peacefully, and when one makes a mistake, the other does not use it to gain the upper hand as individuals in adversarial relationships tend to do. People who relate in cooperative and creative modes show responsibility by doing their duties and by being sensitive to the others' needs.

3. *Adversarial relating.* The partners in an adversarial relationship look out for number one--themselves. They try to get as much from the other while giving as little as possible. The partners are selfish, promote their own self-interests, exploit the other, play one-upmanship, keep score, protect one's own territory, and dominate their own special domains. Each partner worries about falling behind and not getting everything considered rightfully his or hers. They gather evidence, carefully observe any of the other's mistakes, stay ready to defend their interests and to counterattack in case the other encroaches on their territory, and get even in cases of conflict. Such partners may

cooperate in exploiting others or in fighting a common enemy, but that is destructive cooperation.

4. *Antagonistic relating.* An antagonistic relationship feeds on enmity and causes psychological and spiritual damage. The partners hate and abuse each other. They love themselves intensely in many ways, but they hate themselves when they fall short of their glorified self-image and often turn their self-hate into hate of others. They undermine, manipulate, use, and disparage others. These partners show very little compassion, love and caring for others or depth.

In adversarial/antagonistic relationships, the partners keep secrets and do not share much in making decisions. In matters of fairness, these partners tend to use the iron rule of tit for tat rather than the Golden Rule.

Cooperative and creative relationships are consistent with spiritual values while adversarial and antagonistic relationships are not. Spiritual teachers have fostered creative and cooperative relationships as the following story told by the Buddha illustrates. Two acrobats, one a teacher and the other a little girl, were discussing their strategy for safe and efficient performance. The teacher told the young girl that they would watch each other so they could safely perform their feat and make money. But the little girl suggested they each watch themselves carefully and perform their part well so that they could achieve their common goal. The little girl was right, and the teacher had the humility and wisdom to follow her idea. Good team work fosters creative cooperation while teaming up to destroy others fosters destructive cooperation.

There are two types of relationships that Rubin did not touch. They are destructive cooperation and creative competition, both of which are also important to recognize.

5. *Destructive Cooperation.* In destructive cooperation the partners cooperate in a way that is destructive to both partners although one may suffer more than the other. People who enable drug

abusers to keep their addiction are prime examples. Codependents participate actively and passively in harmful and unfair relationships. *Codependency is codestructive.*

Codependent and dependent people become stronger and more self-reliant when they are in close relationship with people of conscience who lovingly set realistic limits and encourage the healthy and discourage the unhealthy aspects of the other. Thus, they become empowered when they have intimate relationships with truly spiritual individuals. On the other hand, dependents and codependents who become close to materialistic individuals tend to be exploited. Authentic spiritual leaders empower their followers, while exploitative leaders seek power, money, and prestige for themselves and discourage the genuine growth of their followers. Subtle exploiters may be the worst because their manipulation is harder to detect.

6. *Creative Competition.* People disagree about the effects of competition. Some experts argue that competition brings out the best in people and cite as example the economic success of Western industrialized nations, especially in comparison to the weak economies the former Soviet Block countries had. Rubin argues that competition brings out the worst in people by promoting paranoia, envy, jealousy, and blocking the healthy growth of the individual. Also, competition leads to focusing on externals, and how to outwit others, and neglect inner development. Competition can damage wisdom and love.

While competition has its benefits in the marketplace, it is often harmful in close human relationships. I believe competition can be useful or harmful, creative or destructive, depending on whether one is using conscience, and therefore using reason, compassion, and love rather than selfishness and meanness. If competition produces constructive results, well and good; if competition produces destructive results, it is clearly undesirable. Good sportsmanship, just as clearly, involves the spirit of creative competition.

In creative competition, creativeness and fairness are emphasized, and the spirit of competition is used to stimulate an additional sense of challenge and excitement. Partners engaged in creative competition channel their energies to enhance their own strength, and they are careful not to take unfair advantage of their partner's weakness.

Thus, cooperative and creative relating is the key to fulfilling relationships, such as happy marriages.

Many personality types tend to relate often in adversarial/antagonistic ways, including destructive competition. A good example of destructive competition is Type A personality with hostility, a person who is in a hurry, driven by the push for success, and easily provoked to anger by trivial frustrations or annoyances. Dr. Redford Williams found that anger and hostility increase risks of coronary heart disease.[37] Studies have also shown that Type As are less successful than Type B's, who are calmer, unhurried, and easy-going. Hostile Type A's harm not only their own heart, but they also cause plenty of heartache and pains for others by their anger, cynicism, and unreasonable suspiciousness. They are difficult people to deal with, especially in any close relationships.

MARITAL RELATIONSHIPS

Dr. John Gottman, author of *Why Marriages Succeed or Fail,* studied more than 2,000 married couples for over two decades and found that the ability to resolve conflicts is a key to lasting marriages. He found three types of healthy marriages on the basis of conflict resolution:

1. *Validating marriages.* These couples discuss problems and work out solutions in a spirit of compromise.

2. *Conflict-avoiding marriages.* These couples avoid confrontation, choosing either to ignore differences, let time heal problems, or one goes along with the other. Their companionship is low.

3. *Volatile marriages.* These couples shows more intense positive and negative emotions; they believe in honesty and expressing their thoughts without much censoring. This approach causes much hurt, but passionate, positive expression of love compensates for the hurt.

Gottman's formula for a stable marriage is to have at least five times as many positive moments as negative ones. He also notes four ways of interacting that damage marriages: criticism that attacks the spouse's character, contempt, defensiveness, and stonewalling. I believe these four ways of interacting are manifestations of adversarial or antagonistic relationships. According to Gottman, couples who avoid conflicts are more likely to value shared religious or ideological beliefs. In my experience, couples who give great importance to a shared philosophy of life are able to overlook less important issues. This can be part of a cooperative or creative relationship rather than unhealthy avoidance. Also, some spouses understand each other well without verbalizing everything. This is especially true in Eastern cultures. While verbalizing is crucial if it promotes better understanding, verbosity that deters understanding can be *boxing matches of chatter boxes.*

In his later book *The Seven Principles For Making Marriage Work,* Gottman notes that a deep friendship is the basis for a happy marriage and friendship protects against adversarial feelings. He warns that couple's discussions that start out harshly would end up in failure and such relationships often fail. His seven principles to make marriage work are: become more aware of each other's personal world, nurture fondness and admiration, turn toward each other instead of away, let your partner influence you, solve your solvable problems, overcome gridlock, and create shared meaning. In my professional and personal experiences, these are the ways partners who are guided by their consciences and a good perspective on human needs relate. On the other hand, bitter divorces with damaging litigation are not rare. Reflecting this situation, as he ended a mock wedding, the priest said: "I declare you future enemies."

RECONCILIATION VERSUS LITIGATION

Many spiritual traditions teach people to refrain from not only wars but also litigation except in extreme situations; they encourage people to seek negotiated settlement and reconciliation instead. Confucius' ideals have strongly influenced Chinese culture for centuries to value negotiations, compromises, and mediations.

Gandhi, although a lawyer by education, vigorously promoted cooperative/creative relating even with adversaries. Harivallabh Parikh, a follower of Gandhi in India, has settled more than 50,000 cases ranging from marital disputes to murders by reconciliation through arbitration. In many cases, Parikh has ended cycles of violence and vengeance by reconciling the enemies. The former chief justice of India has praised Parikh's service even though it is outside the official judicial system. Parikh's techniques may not exactly suit other cultures, but the underlying principles can be adapted.

There is a legitimate place for litigation, especially when other approaches fail to achieve fair solutions. But when the role of litigation is taken to extremes, it fosters a destructive adversarial/antagonistic spirit. As the Taoists teach, when one thing is taken to its extreme, it becomes the opposite; when claims of justice are taken to extremes, they really become injustice.

CONSCIENCE AND RELATIONSHIPS

Ignorance and lack of empathy damage the functioning of conscience in promoting healthy relationships. If we know and empathize with the needs of others, we can really apply the Golden Rule in our relationships. Every working day I sadly observe the tragic deficiency in many people's openness to knowledge, empathy, and willingness to act fairly. If we live by our consciences, we will relate in cooperative and creative ways. Adversarial and antagonistic, especially antagonistic relating is caused by deficiency in empathy, compassion, and love; such deficiency is connected with distorted views about oneself, others, and life.

The teaching of Jesus to love our enemies has practical limitations; we cannot love our enemies without sufficient safeguards, but we can use our consciences and be fair and responsible in dealing with them. From a purely psychological view, it is right for people to act according to the level of meanness and hate their societies endorse. But to be spiritually healthy, we must use conscience, not simply society's values. Many religious and social groups that claim to believe in the Golden Rule do not practice it; instead, they promote narrow outlooks and distorted impressions about others.

If we utilize our consciences properly, our relationships will be healthy. This approach has worked successfully for many of my patients, including Chris and Christy. When they met over a decade ago she was lonely because several men had rejected her due to her diabetes which was not well-controlled then. Chris accepted her, and they became intimate. Having a temper, he would mouth off but was not physically violent. They married, had two children, and established a business together. Christy's diabetes was well controlled, and she helped Chris in business. The stress of running their business and Chris's drinking excessively off and on prompted arguments, and their relationship became increasingly adversarial. As Chris became verbally abusive more frequently, Christy and he began to talk about divorce. When I first saw them, they focused on each other's faults. In individual sessions later, I encouraged each of them to talk about their own strengths and weaknesses as well as the other person's strengths. Then I helped them put their current conflicts into the overall context of their relationship in the past and its potential for the future. I urged them to use their consciences and understand and help to fulfill each other's needs. As they tried this, with therapy for a few months, their marriage became happy.

Widespread conflicts and breakups of families is a reflection of people not living by their consciences. To use conscience properly, we have to be aware of our defenses, especially projection of our own ideas onto other people. Some couples in conflict act like the partner is as bad as a demon. In attempting to shock one such couple into reality, I asked: "Did the two of you meet in hell?" The question helped them some but their marriage was beyond repair, and we had to focus on minimizing damages of divorce.

Often people think of projection as "reading" something bad in others (envy, for example) that is not really there, but projection can be about highly desirable qualities that are absent. When we are infatuated with a person, including ourselves, we may imagine wonderful qualities that are nonexistent. It is crucial to be a keen observer and a fair judge of our perceptions, interpretations, and responses.

Excessive feelings of attachment or aversion can confuse our judgment and damage our spiritual balance, and so freedom from such intense feelings is useful. According to a story a Buddhist monk took a precious picture with him when he left China for Japan. The picture depicted a great Buddhist monk burning Buddhist scriptures when he attained enlightenment, thereby giving up excessive attachment to the tool he had used in his spiritual growth. Often we get too attached or averse to objects and ideas based on past experiences and future expectations.

Fairness in relationships includes giving reasonable time for the other person to change. Time after time I have seen relationships end just when one of the partners is finally changing for the better, often because the partner who has been grinning and bearing the problems for so long gave up at a very crucial time. For instance, Marie who had not gotten her needs for attention and affection met by her husband, kept complaining and building up her resentment for many years. He kept ignoring her until she started divorce proceedings; then he opened his eyes and finally got involved in therapy. The woman questioned his sincerity and proceeded with the divorce without giving him what I felt was a reasonable chance to prove that he had changed.

According to an Indian saying, we have to rub the gold against a touchstone to see its true quality, and the natural rub that occurs in crisis often reveals many secrets about relationships and the personality of the partners. Using our consciences we can exercise our wisdom and love in the crisis to strengthen ourselves and others.

Conscience can guide us in our choices and help keep healthy relationships to ourselves, others, the natural world, and God. That truly is a formula for fulfillment.

8. BE POWERFUL AND FREE

"He who overcomes others has force;He who overcomes himself is strong."[38]

Lao Tzu

The word "power" is derived from the Latin *posse* which means "to be able." To fulfill our hearts and souls, we need the ability to deal well with our many needs. We can develop the powers of imagination, reason, and will, and live with the greatest of human powers, namely, love and wisdom.

POWER AND TRUE OR FALSE PERCEPTION OF IT

We can use both real and perceived power in healthy or unhealthy ways. A story told by the Buddha illustrates the false sense of power resulting from intoxication. A beetle wandering in the forest came upon some alcohol, feasted on it, and got drunk. As the intoxicated beetle moved on, it wandered onto an elephant's path. A male elephant saw the beetle and moved out of the way to prevent hurting it. The beetle thought the elephant moved away out of fear and wanting to prove its power all the more, insisted on fighting with the elephant. The elephant still did not want to harm the beetle but decided to teach the arrogant creature a good lesson. So he turned around and dropped a ball of feces on the hardheaded insect. Here the story ends, but my imagination is that the drunken beetle thought, "I scared the feces out of that elephant." The morning after, when the insolent insect sobered up and crawled out of the feces, it probably reassessed the experience and gained insight from the free reality therapy given by the elephant. The elephant, knowing his real power, had no need to prove his power to others, and he was compassionate.

Alcohol, drugs, addictive relationships, and unhealthy pride can give us a false sense of power, causing us to act foolishly. A false sense of power may be based on an exaggerated importance of certain positions, possessions, skills, and relationships to powerful people. One way psychological and spiritual defenses work is by providing a false sense of power.

Another form of false sense of power is denial of powerlessness. Addicts often do not realize how powerless they are over their addiction. Therefore, the first step of AA is admitting one's powerlessness over alcohol. Some people have the opposite distortion, a perception of powerlessness when they really have power. By not recognizing and using their power, they often lose it.

It is often said that power corrupts because people tend to abuse their powers. Powerlessness can also cause corruption by limiting our choices in meeting our needs. Destructive use of power towards oneself and others in various degrees is a common problem.

POWER AND POWERLESSNESS CORRUPT

In a Greek myth the boy Icarus abused his ability to fly using his wings of wax; flying too close to the sun, the wax melted and he fell into the sea. From overeating to self-mutilation and suicide, there are numerous self-destructive uses of powers. Many people abuse others, specially the stronger or meaner people exploit or harm others who are in a weaker position. Abuse of children by some adults and exploitation of followers by certain leaders are examples of such corruption. The abusers meet various needs such as power, pleasure, and esteem in this way. Many self-mutilators (who deliberately injure themselves) have told me that they get a sense of power and relief when they injure themselves, as if being on the cutting edge of life.

Moreover, many individuals use unethical means including legal and illegal violence and pressure to gain and maintain power. Brute force and threats of violence are commonly used by antisocial personalities, gangs, machos, and totalitarian governments to make people obey. Likewise, clever sales tactics and legal manipulations are used by many, especially by slick people, to get their way.

A sense of power and prestige in being part of "high society" and "fast life" caused several of my patients to become drug addicts. Then, to support their drug habits they started stealing and lying. In many cases, these led to divorce, job loss, depression, suicide attempts, and rapid departure of "fast life" friends.

While the above ways of power corrupting someone is easy to grasp, it is harder to understand why powerlessness corrupts. Powerlessness corrupts because of the helplessness and hopelessness that the powerless person feels. In a state of dependence and desperation, people are more likely to participate in unethical behavior than if they had a healthy sense of power. Those who cleverly abuse power often find it easy to prey on the weak. Powerlessness is a major reason women become workers in the sex industry which employs call girls and prostitutes. Since the economic decline of the former Soviet Union, tens of thousands of women from that region have been trafficked to the global sex industry.

Powerlessness is behind several forms of destructive relationships--from the worker who stays in a poorly paid job to the badly battered wife who feels powerless to leave her husband. Common people in feudalistic societies had very little political and economic power, but in democratic countries we expect the masses to enjoy significant political and economic power. But in reality, powerful special interest groups diminish the power of the masses.

The sense of powerlessness of some people is cleverly manipulated by others. For instance, some groups attract others to join them by stirring up a sense of powerlessness. Cult leaders usually wield unhealthy power over their relatively powerless followers who relinquish much of their power by blindly following their cult's ideology.

Many people avoid using their powers because they are afraid that the very use of power may lead them in the wrong direction. For instance, many people do not use their capacity for reason, imagination, and empathy to go beyond their social conditioning. They are too scared, not prudent, and fail to understand that they can learn to overcome such fears. One can face fears gradually, take small steps in using more power, evaluate the results, and proceed further if the results are useful or stop otherwise.

The cliché, "if you don't use it, you lose it" is true in many ways. For example, if we don't use the power of love and wisdom, we can very well lose these two most important abilities. People who use excessive defenses become less capable of using their capacities for love and wisdom; individuals with severe personality disorders are prime examples of this.

Former Chinese leader Mao Tze Tung's famous statement that power grows out of the barrel of a gun has become a tragic reality in many parts of the world. There are people who use violence to meet various needs--physical needs including sex, self-esteem, security, pleasure, and identity. Many such people consider violent behavior as right and proper. Therefore, they do not even have guilt and shame to control aggressive behavior. External pressure becomes necessary to control the behavior of such people. Violent behavior, except when really needed for self-defense, goes against our conscience. But violence may be sanctioned and promoted by the superego of people who are socially conditioned to believe in aggression. Violent programs on television have been shown to increase aggressive behavior of some viewers. Those who argue that even great Shakespearean and Greek tragedies portray violence are missing the point. The violent actions in classical tragedies are not glamorized as in modern television, but are presented in ways that stimulate the conscience of the audience and create disgust for violence.

Obviously, many people go to extremes with their need for power. Several possible reasons for this extremism are: 1) More power can enhance self-esteem and esteem from others. 2) Those with more power and prestige have a better chance for brighter future for themselves and their heirs. 3) Power offers better chances for various pleasures. 4) In most societies, the powerful have a greater chance of maintaining and acquiring more power, as the saying goes: "Winner take all and devil take the hindmost." 5) For many individuals, their possessions and positions of power are important aspects of identity, and the more power they have the stronger their identity. 6) There are religious people who consider material power as evidence of divine blessing; the more material power they have, the more blessed they feel. They may also feel that the powerless are blessed out by God and relish a sense of superiority over the weak. 7) Those who grew up feeling powerless tend to feel especially good when they gain power. 8) The power of individuals reinforces the power of the group. So many people support their leaders who use unfair means to gain and maintain power because it suits their own selfish purpose. 9) Many people make the attainment of material power the source of meaning in their lives. 10) The powerful have far better chance of meeting physical needs. 11) Sense of power can enhance one's libido. Some claim that power is the best aphrodisiac.

HEALTHY POWER

The powers of love and wisdom are always healthy, but the power of will and imagination can be used in healthy or unhealthy ways. When we use our physical, psychological, and spiritual powers in promoting our own and others' well-being, we are fulfilling our hearts and souls. Power used in harmony with our conscience is consistently healthy. Our capacities for love and wisdom are our most precious powers, and love and wisdom reinforce each other.

THE POWER OF LOVE AND WISDOM

The power of love and wisdom can grow even in the midst of adversities as Diane, who suffered from depression and marital problems, showed. Diane and her husband David had many good things going for them; he was financially successful and she was beautiful and sociable. Diane's depression with many ups and downs was partly caused by conflicts with David who has a strong tendency to control Diane and put her down. He discouraged her social interests and almost daily found fault with her for something. Couples therapy failed because David totally denied his problems. Diane's self-esteem and sense of power were low; she had limited her life to suit her husband and did very little with her own talents.

Assertiveness, withdrawal, talk of divorce, and therapy all failed to change David's behavior. For various reasons Diane did not want a divorce. Diane had grown up in a peaceful family. Also, her rigid and narrow religious background had limited her psychological and spiritual understanding. She felt powerless and stuck. Although her medications fairly controlled her clinical depression, she had not dealt with the issues of her powerlessness, low self-esteem, and overall unhappy life. As we worked on these issues she made several changes that made her life much more fulfilling than before: she learned to use her creative abilities more, relate with people who have similar interests, and she began to use her conscience which lifted her self-esteem, rather than use her superego which caused unhealthy guilt. Diane accepted that David was unlikely to change, but she realized she did not have to take his unfair criticism seriously. She expanded her wisdom by reading materials on psychological and spiritual health. She is among many who grew up in happy families and found themselves lost in their relationship to selfish partners. Wisdom for such people who grew up in good families includes a realistic insight into the bad side of life.

The power of love and wisdom along with discipline can often help to rescue teenagers who are getting deeper into rebellion, resentment, and hate. A sense of powerlessness causes some people to rebel unwisely and make matters worse, and teenagers are particularly prone to this problem. In my experience, reinforcing any love bond and helping to keep the teenager's mind open are very important for their progress. Take the case of George who was brought up by his divorced mother with very few rules. He had done fairly well until his mother remarried and set ground rules. George disliked his stepfather and his mother's rules, and rebelled both actively and passively. His grades fell, he blamed others, and complained frequently. After making progress initially in therapy, his problems worsened as his mother and stepfather punished him for disobedience.

George misinterpreted his mother's motives; he saw her as a mean and unloving person who was getting pleasure out of hurting him. As I noticed his attitudes getting increasingly defensive and hateful, I was able to help him by three approaches: 1) I suggested to his mother to do everything possible to show love, and to show her sadness, not just anger, when he hurt her feelings. She had both feelings but expressed only anger, since she thought expressing sadness was a sign of weakness. 2) I got active involvement of his grandmother who he felt always loved him. 3) I tried to keep his mind open to the possibility that his mother cared even if she did not show it the way he wished. These approaches worked in turning George's life around to a loving and productive one, whereas earlier behavioral approaches of reward and punishment had failed.

St. Paul's famous statement about love (1 Corinthians: 4-7) gives an interesting list of many elements of love. It is enduring, kind, unselfish and unfailing; it rejoices in truth and bears, believes, and hopes all things; it does not envy, show off or behave rudely; and it does not rejoice in evil. The power of love is the capacity to   nurture and realistically protect ourselves and others, and it promotes cooperative and creative modes of relating.

The power of love is also the best antidote for the love of power which often causes adversarial and antagonistic relationships. In loving genuinely and deeply, we are *sharing* our powers with the ones we love, empowering the other, sacrificing our interests when necessary, and enjoying giving the beloved various degrees of power. Those who have an excessive need for power and control have difficulty in loving; they lack the wisdom to realize that they cannot really find fulfillment by meeting their greed for power.

The power of wisdom comes with its depth of vision and understanding, openness of mind, and a balance between the rational and the emotional aspects of ourselves. Wisdom involves knowing realistic limits, and an understanding of what deserves attention and what can be overlooked. Such pragmatic understanding promotes inner peace by enabling us to accept realistic limits.

Love and wisdom utilize the powers of will and imagination in the healthy direction. Therefore, before we apply our power of will and imagination, we need to use conscience to examine whether our choices are healthy.

A healthy mode of generating and channeling our power is pursuing a good goal with enthusiasm. Imagination is a great source to generate enthusiasm. If our imagination is on all the positive (attractive) aspects of our goal--imagining both the process of achieving the goal and the benefits from it--then our motivation will be strong. If our imagination focuses on all the problems associated with the goal, then our enthusiasm, and our willpower, will be weak.

POWER OF WILL AND IMAGINATION

Willpower is our voluntary capacity to act in accordance with our goals and ideals. Many individuals who want to give up a bad habit or develop a good habit fail to achieve their goal because of poor willpower. Some people are confused about the difference between willpower and power of imagination, but a few simple examples can clarify the confusion. For instance, when we want to make a fist, we do it using our willpower. Our so-called "voluntary muscles" follow our will, and so we can use our willpower to control these muscles, but when we want our mouth to water, we can use our imagination--imagine we are eating lemon. Similarly, a healthy man can get an erection by using sexual fantasy, but not by giving a military command "Stand at attention" to his male organ.

Willpower involves making choices and keeping commitment. Practice of meditation and other spiritual and physical exercises strengthens willpower by exercising right choices and commitments. For instance, in twenty minutes of meditation, we exercise the right choice (of letting distractions go) numerous times, and practicing meditation regularly reinforces commitment. Both enhance willpower.

Visualization exercises help much to strengthen our imaginative capacity. Imagine yourself enjoying a wonderful relaxation at a beach or another setting you like. Imagine the various sights, sounds, sense of touch, smell, and taste you enjoy in that setting and how it is making your body and mind relax (see more in Appendix). Listening to audiotapes of visualization practice and reading fiction and poetry can also help strengthen imagination. The powers of will and imagination reinforce each other. You can keep thoughts and feelings that are useful for you and let the harmful thoughts and feelings go. Thus, you can exercise your will (by repeatedly making the correct choice) and your imaginative capacity (by choosing mental images that support and enhance the pursuit of your goal). To illustrate, if you are a smoker who wants to quit smoking, use your imagination about all the benefits of being a non-smoker; don't keep imagining how much you miss smoking.

We can make our willpower more effective by utilizing strong wish and hope, repeating practice, and rewarding ourselves and getting others to reward us for desirable behavior. By stimulating strong wishes to achieve a goal, we can add much energy to our will; and we can use our imagination to strengthen our wish. Similarly, we can generate good hope by our reason and imagination, and by the examples of people who have overcome adversities or realized their potential in admirable ways.

If we repeatedly use our will and imagination in accordance with our goals it becomes our habit. Habits are second nature to us which means we automatically tend to act according to our habit. Regular practice of physical and spiritual exercises helps us greatly to be self-disciplined or to be able to use our will properly instead of being driven by our impulses. Thus, a person with spiritually healthy habits automatically tends to do what is consistent with spiritual values. Such an individual who has overcome his or her selfishness and impulsiveness is truly strong. Still we are human and may have weaknesses especially based on certain bad experiences or influences in our lives. We need to be cautious about the weak points in ourselves and compassionate about them in others. One of the great insights in Shakespearean and other classic tragedies is that the hero with many great qualities and a weakness, a *tragic* flaw, is not considered a hypocrite but a hero.

Reinforcements and rewards from ourselves and others are also quite useful to enhance our willpower. We can often just use our imagination to give ourselves enough good strokes to maintain healthy willpower.

SECURITY AND FREEDOM

A significant part of our power lies in security and freedom. A sense of security or freedom from danger and deprivation is a result of several factors: 1) physical security of law and order in society, 2) financial security of job, insurance, and the like, 3) psychological security of emotional strength, support systems, 4) spiritual security of living meaningfully by one's conscience.

Emotional as well as spiritual conflicts cause insecurity. In order to relieve the anxiety of insecurity, we may do things that make matters even worse. An example is that of Cindy who grew up in a dysfunctional family and later married an unfaithful man. She stayed in the relationship for five years, hoping and praying that he would change his ways. When he did not, she divorced him. A couple of years later, she fell in love with a caring and dependable man she had known for many years. They married after dating for nearly a year. Then, gradually Cindy started actively searching for any possible evidence that her husband was cheating on her. Her husband was understanding of her insecurity to a great extent, but her increasingly baseless suspicion of him began to strain their relationship. With her husband's support Cindy got therapy and overcame her excessive insecurity which was a carryover from her first marriage. Had she not gotten help and changed her behavior, her marriage would have ended, causing her to become even more insecure.

While conflicts within the individual can be a significant cause of insecurity, major conflicts within one's family, community and country also shake one's security. The more insecurity the more defensive the individual, which means more energies are spent in protective measures and less energy is spent for nurturing (as we saw in Chapter Four). There are people who have suffered food shortage years ago who feel insecure unless they have several freezers full of food stored up. Victims of war may continue to suffer intense insecurity even when they are living in peaceful situations. Besides war, the prevalence of violence, corruption, and litigiousness in society causes realistic insecurity for people who do not want to be victimized by, or profit from, such problems. When many conflicts and uncertainties go on in society, people often reduce their insecurity by focusing on the areas over which they feel control. During war people may overlook what is going on just a few miles away and focus on their immediate surroundings.

Individuals and communities have obligations to each other to promote security for all, and many issues of security need to be dealt with by communities as a whole. Spiritually healthy people cannot feel satisfied by protecting themselves with alarm systems, weapons, and insurance policies for themselves while ignoring the needs of others; rather, the protection of others is also of concern for them. The powerless or the underdogs of society can achieve power in healthy ways by developing their own physical, spiritual and psychological strengths, and by cooperative and creative support among themselves.

FREEDOM

Freedom is so dear to us that many would prefer death to the lack of freedom. We love our social and political freedom and freedom from sickness. Religious freedom is crucial for a great many individuals, as has been shown by numerous immigrants who fled religious persecution in their countries, taking enormous risks to reach the United States. People often miss the significance of many psychological and spiritual freedoms, such as the freedom to think freely, understand deeply and face reality. It is very sad when people do not develop their capacity for reason, love, imagination, will, empathy, and conscience.

Individuals whose thinking is twisted and whose growth is stunted by the heavy sales pitch of the market place and the propaganda of the religious, political, and other ideological extremists are really enslaved. What freedom do we truly have if our thoughts and feelings are in chains and our conscience is given wrong information? The Grand Inquisitor in Dostoevsky's The *Brothers Karamazov* claims that people want authority, miracle, and mystery, not freedom. Erich Fromm in *Escape From Freedom*--which someone said he wrote after he divorced his wife Freida--notes how people escape from freedom by submitting to authority, destructiveness, or automaton conformity.

POWER AND TOUGHNESS

One important aspect of power is toughness, and toughness is a big issue in many cultures including the United States. There is much talk about tough guys vs. softies, strong men vs. weaklings, macho vs. wimp, and so on. People do interesting, useful, wasteful, foolish, and even harmful things to appear tough. Genuine toughness is not roughness but strength involving capacity for endurance and empathy, courage and compassion, hardiness and heart.
The main features of healthy and sick toughness are:

HEALTHY TOUGHNESS	SICK TOUGHNESS
Strong willpower for good purpose	Strong willpower for evil or selfish purpose
Does not block out or diminish realistic guilt/shame	Blocks or diminishes realistic guilt/shame
Shows compassion and patience	Low in compassion/patience
Healthy persistence	Stubbornness
Avoids violence if possible	Enjoys show of force
Shows tenderness	Deficient in tenderness
Shows wisdom	Shows lack of wisdom
Shows healthy identity	Shows unhealthy identity

A cruel and hateful person, like Joseph Stalin, and a compassionate and loving person, like Mother Teresa, have shown tremendous toughness in this century. In one sense, the toughest people are the most hardened criminals, the daredevils who do things which make normal people feel sick. But the little Mother Teresas who endure long hardships because of their compassion and love are also very tough. There is no question which kind of toughness is healthy and desirable. Obviously, the toughness of the criminal is a weakness in disguise although criminal groups with their deranged values admire it as strength.

POWER, FREEDOM, AND CONSCIENCE

Conscience guides us to use our powers and freedoms to make our lives fulfilling. But superego may misguide a person to abuse power or to refrain from using appropriate power, based on social conditioning.

People who use conscience regularly, keep their feelings in control and their thinking rational based on broad perspective. This frees the person of conscience from excessive feelings and irrational thinking and consequent irrational or irresponsible behavior. Conscience guides us to maintain physical, emotional, and spiritual health by making good choices in these matters.

Making choices to maintain physical health is a crucial part of living by one's conscience. Such choices include healthy diet, exercise, hygiene, sufficient sleep, avoidance of physically harmful choices, and following appropriate treatment when sick.

Healthy use of power is important in relationships. A couple in their thirties had problems related to power in their relationship. Ben did not exercise his power sufficiently, and Brenda abused her power. Ben felt guilty about opposing Brenda when she was unfair to him because his superego demanded that he should please his wife. Brenda had grown up in a violent family and acted violently toward Ben many times when she got drunk. With therapy, Ben learned that his guilt about setting reasonable limits with Brenda was coming from his unhealthy superego, and that he could use his conscience and be lovingly assertive with her. Brenda learned to use her conscience and feel realistic guilt about her violence and alcohol abuse, instead of letting her superego keep approving her violence. She also benefited from AA which reinforced her use of conscience.

If we live by the guidance of conscience, we can experience an authentic sense of inner strength, which enhances inner peace and supports courage. Conscience discourages unnecessary power struggles, prohibits destructive and exploitative use of power, but encourages pursuit of power through love and wisdom. When we exercise our powers--physical, mental, social, and spiritual--with love and wisdom, we are at our best and we can experience joy. Everyday we can find plenty of opportunities to do so.

9. INTEGRATE YOUR PAST

"Forgiveness is not the alternative to revenge because it is soft and gentle; *it is a viable alternative because it is the only creative route to less unfairness.*" [39]

Lewis B. Smedes

Given our long-term memory and our need to evaluate our experiences, we have to deal with our past. Our choice is between either using our past to promote love and wisdom and thereby enhance our fulfillment, or letting our past damage our present and future. Healthy integration of the past is very useful for leading a fulfilling life as it helps us:

- see the reality of current situations without being distorted by past experiences
- have clear and healthy direction for the future
- prevent excessive psychological or spiritual defenses based on the past
- use our energy and potential for being our best
- prevent being stuck in a victim role or being caught up in vengeance

HEALTHY AND UNHEALTHY LESSONS FROM THE PAST

Many people are pessimistic about trying something new because it has not been tested and proven. When Mahatma Gandhi began his non-violent political struggle for India's freedom from Britain, a prominent Indian historian tried to dissuade him by pointing out that never before in history had any nation gained freedom without violence. Gandhi, observing that history teaches that new things do happen, pursued nonviolent political activism and achieved his goal. Since then, non-violent political struggles in various parts of the world have brought great progress in freedom, peace, and social justice. Billions of people have benefited from Gandhi's taking the right lesson from history.

Throughout the ages, various religions and spiritual groups have emphasized the importance of proper training of children to shape their personality in the right way. From Freud's psychoanalytic theories to John Bradshaw's ideas on healing the wounded inner child, there have been numerous works about how childhood experiences shape our lives.

What may be traumatic to a child may not be obvious abuse or neglect but more subtle actions that can have lasting impact too. The case of an anorgasmic woman is illustrative. Her father, a religious and caring person, was frequently physically affectionate toward her until an incident when she was about six years old. She was sitting in his lap and they were hugging each other, and she was kissing him. When she started kissing his ear, he suddenly became uncomfortable and put her down. Since then, he avoided showing much physical affection towards her but continued to be loving otherwise. She grew up having problems with intimacy and never experienced orgasm. In therapy, she realized that her father who showed a strict superego, probably got scared by some sexual stimulation he may have experienced when she kissed his ear. Reacting with excessive caution since then, his reaction led her to be scared of intimacy. With this insight, she gradually enjoyed intimacy with her husband and became orgasmic.

Being able to deal with negative experiences, as well as to enjoy and incorporate positive ones, is very much a part of psychological and spiritual strength. The saying that experience is the best teacher requires some qualifications. We may get the right or wrong impression from our experiences, use correct or incorrect evaluation, and learn true or false lessons from the same experience. Experience is the best teacher only if we learn the right lesson; but often the lesson learned is wrong and it results in various misperceptions about oneself, others, and life.

Psychologist Martin Seligman's research on learned helplessness[40] illustrates how wrong lessons can be learned from experience. Seligman gave mild electric shock to one group of dogs but gave them some control over the shock, e.g., by pushing a panel with their nose the dogs could stop the shock. Another group of dogs had no way of controlling or escaping from the shock, they were helpless. Interestingly, when the helpless group was given a chance to escape the shock later, they did not use the opportunity. They had given up on the basis of their previous experience. Seligman has observed similar learned helplessness in depressed patients. Psychotherapy often involves helping people to unlearn faulty lessons from their past.

REPEAT OLD TRAUMAS OR USE THE CHANCES TO HEAL

Corrective emotional experience is an emotionally good experience that corrects the traumatic influence of past experiences. This insight promoted by Psychoanalyst Franz Alexander in the 1940's did not become popular but the idea is very useful. Many of the wounds in life caused by bad experiences are healed by good experiences later.

What often blocks a person from using corrective emotional experience is excessive defensiveness and pessimistic outlook that prevents the victim from trying the possibilities of good experiences. For example, Peggy divorced her domineering and unfaithful husband after five years of an unhappy relationship. Since then, she has put her heart and soul into her work, and blocked out any chances for romantic relationships. She kept herself busy and never reflected on anything missing in her life. Later, when she became unhappy with her work, she realized it was a big mistake to have given up male companionship.

Freud's idea of repetition compulsion (a compulsion to repeat certain experiences and situations from the earlier part of one's life) has gained much popularity. Psychotherapists often look for such tendencies in their clients. For example, a man who was abused and dominated by his mother repeatedly chose female partners who are abusive and domineering. Gaining this insight in therapy helped him to overcome the unhealthy pattern. It is important to gain insight into such repetition of one's history, but the similar importance due for corrective emotional experience seems to be often missed in therapy.

Take the case of Ellen who was emotionally and sexually abused by her father. Later she lived in a traumatic situation of an abusive marriage for many years. Her husband berated her often, used her financially and sexually, and controlled her social life. At work, she came to closely know a male colleague who was sensitive, kind, and nurturing. He was having marital problems and had discussed seriously with his wife his plans for separation and divorce. Ellen and Ed became romantically involved while both of them were struggling in their respective marriages. Ellen's love for Ed and his emotional and financial support made her feel strong and special. She came alive as a woman with esteem, power, and a stronger identity. With Ed's support, she was able to break off from her husband. However, Ed's ambivalence about his marriage continued particularly because he had young children. Ellen was distressed that Ed did not divorce, but she noticed his genuine struggle and caring for her.

Her earlier therapies had focused on Ellen's relationship to abusive men and interpreted her relationship with Ed as just a repetition of victimhood. She could not accept this interpretation as it overlooked the many positive (corrective) experiences she was getting in her relationship with Ed. As we looked at the positive aspects of her romantic relationship (her sense of being lovable, sexy, special, and powerful) along with the negative aspects of staying in an uncommitted relationship, she felt much better and was able to break off and move on.

In many relationships aspects of both repetition compulsion and corrective emotional experience are present. Awareness of these two issues helps one to discard the unhealthy and keep the healthy aspects of the relationship, and thus relate well to the other person while integrating one's own past. If the relationship remains sick, then one can use one's conscience and move on peacefully.

I find it far more beneficial to actively encourage patients to pursue healing and growth experiences than to focus excessively on past traumas. After talking about the traumas, letting feelings out, clarifying who was responsible and the likely need that person was meeting, it is better to focus on finding balance at present and moving on to better future. Therapy focused too intensely and for too long on past traumas seems to slow or prevent healing. Often the traumas result from growing up in dysfunctional families. Such children do not necessarily become dysfunctional; they may become strong survivors.

VERY DIFFERENT IMPACTS OF DYSFUNCTIONAL FAMILIES

It is well known that children of dysfunctional families often tend to develop various problems including low self-esteem, insecurity, addictions, depression, and relationship and sexual problems. Much less known is the fact that many children from dysfunctional families become strong individuals. It is important to have empathy and compassion for the suffering victims of dysfunctional families, but it is also extremely useful to learn about the resilient individuals, the strong survivors of such families. The features of resilience deserve to be understood, encouraged, and emulated.

Steven and Sybil Wolin in their book *The Resilient Self* identify seven factors in resilience. The Wolins emphasize that *morality* is the most important feature of resilience. Resilient children use their conscience, utilize the moral energy, and do what is right. They preserve their goodness and reject the unhealthy example of their parents or other authority figures. They also tend to fight unfairness in their family and outside. This is very much true in my clinical and personal experience.

Other features of resilient individuals are *initiative* and *independence* (exploring new possibilities and pursuing their own goals), *relationships* to healthy adults, developing *insight* into their situation, sense of *humor* (to reduce suffering and relate better to others), and *creativity*. Creativity involves using imagination and intelligence and shaping something out of chaos.

Even in the same dysfunctional family, children who are resilient often make use of opportunity for support from good neighbors or others while children who are not resilient may not utilize the same opportunity. A colleague of mine confided that she grew up in a very dysfunctional family but found a real home with her husband's family which helped to heal her old wounds.

I have given resilience much importance because it shows the human capacity for using intelligence guided by conscience in meeting one's needs, even in very difficult situations, and the benefits of it. Those people who were abused and did not go in the resilient direction, can still learn to use the beneficial approaches of resilience.   Resilience deserves far more attention in the mental health profession and in the mass media than it has gotten.

FORGIVENESS AND RECONCILIATION

In our attempts to integrate the past, we have to face what to do with those who have hurt us--whether to forgive or not, or whether to reconcile or not. If someone has hurt us, we can keep fuming about it or put out the fires of anger and resentment and channel our energies usefully.

One way many people attempt to overcome their hurt is by taking revenge, a theme common in popular culture. From a purely psychological view, any degree of revenge that is legally safe is fine. There is psychological pleasure and satisfaction in sweet revenge, and a sense of more power in going beyond retaliation to extra punishment--a whole mouthful of teeth for one tooth.

Obsession with past hurt and wish for vengeance can, however, keep people psychologically and spiritually stuck in an unhealthy state. Take the case of Jack who had chronic insomnia for twenty years because of his grudge against his former friend Larry who had seduced his wife Jan. At the time of the affair, Jack was newly married, worked long hours, and spent very little time with his wife. Larry used his abundant leisure time to charm Jan who was lonely. In a few weeks Jan felt guilty, broke off the affair, and told Jack about it. Jack took out some of his anger on her.

Although Larry had moved away and Jack did not go after him, Jack gradually became obsessed about the episode and felt ashamed that he did not take revenge on Larry. He wanted to kill Larry or at least beat him up badly. Jack's faith would not let him carry out his wish for revenge. He sought psychiatric help a few times over the years, but it did not help him significantly, and so he went on suffering.

The following approaches worked well in resolving Jack's problem: 1) Jack was encouraged to understand the confusion in his values (conflict between spiritual value opposing and cultural value promoting vengeance). 2) He was shown how to raise his self-esteem by using his conscience and spiritual values. 3) He was helped to understand the reasons for the affair (Jack was not meeting Jan's needs and she did not confront him about it because of her lack of assertiveness, and Larry met her needs; Jan was not using her conscience for a while). 4) He was helped to appreciate Jan's awakened conscience, genuine guilt, and her love for him. 5) He was taught how to focus his attention away from the past hurt to the good things in his life and in their marriage now, as well as future potential. 6) Jack was encouraged to strengthen all his loving relationships. 7) His belief in divine justice and in spirituality in general were utilized to support these steps. Hypnosis was also used to help him relax deeply and let go of the past and focus on the present and future.

Forgiveness is like writing off a bad debt or throwing out something from our storage because it is no longer useful and is wasting space. In fact, strong negative feelings and memories associated with a past experience are more like a poison which causes damage if we don't get rid of it. With this intention, we can forgive even without cooperation from the person who hurt us.

Reconciliation is like doing business again; and reestablishing a broken relationship requires the cooperation of the person who hurt us. Also it involves changes in the other person or often on the part of both to make a new and improved relationship.

If we are estranged from ourselves, forgiveness is not enough, we have to reconcile and relate to ourselves to enjoy fulfilling lives. Of course, we have to deal with our guilt or shame realistically to reconcile.

In trying to reconcile with others, first we have to explore any wish to do what is right, the possibility of developing an understanding of what happened with a vision for some common good in the future. The offender needs to listen to and understand the victim's suffering, soothe the victim's negative feelings, and provide assurances that the hurt will not be repeated. Simple promises such as "I won't do it again" are not enough; offenders have to show how their attitudes and actions have really changed and what specifically they would do to prevent repetition of the wrongs. At the same time, victims have to be willing to understand the offenders' side too and try to cooperate in building a mutually beneficial future.

False pride, a wrong sense of power and security, and close-mindedness are common obstacles to forgiveness and reconciliation. Victimizers often keep a false pride by denying or minimizing the harm done to the victim or use arguments to wrongly support their wrongs. Victims may also use false pride and prevent guilt about not trying to forgive or reconcile.

Some people have a false pride about not forgiving themselves. One perfectionist kept badgering himself for every little fault and remained depressed. On many occasions when I asked him why he wouldn't forgive himself from the past and move forward, he would say, "I will not lower my standard." He was sickly proud of his superego's unrealistic standard, but gradually he opened his mind to how harmful it was and accepted a fair standard of conscience. Then his self-esteem and his depression improved.

Insecurity holds some people back from forgiving. These individuals derive a false sense of security or power by holding on to hurt and anger. For example, Tip, who was rigid, compulsive, and moralistic, found it very difficult to forgive Tanya for a romantic indiscretion. Tanya was a sensitive, imaginative, and emotional person with strong need for attention, affection, and freedom. Tip's personality did not allow him to meet Tanya's needs well. They had a common friend Al with whom Tanya could speak freely on many subjects. Tanya and Al expressed affection but had no sex. Tip found out and became furious, and Tanya felt very guilty and broke off her friendship with Al. Tip could not forgive her and kept badgering her verbally off and on for months. In therapy, we focused on his deep insecurity and rigid values, and how he could become psychologically and spiritually stronger.

Tip had a very strict, punitive upbringing, and was guided by a rigid, harsh superego. His rigidity gave him a false sense of security. He feared that if he forgave Tanya, she would be more likely to repeat her behavior. He also realized that if he kept on badgering her, she might eventually get fed up and leave him. Tip slowly recognized that his values were based on fear and punishment, not on love. Having not experienced deep love as he was growing up, in his marriage too his love was tainted by his excessive need for control. So I pointed out to him the opportunity presented by this crisis for him to use his conscience, instead of his unhealthy superego to guide him, to be more loving and lovable. Gradually he accepted that he could trust his wife on a new basis of deeper understanding that they could meet each other's needs far better than they had done before. In the past his trust was based on unrealistic ideals of Tanya, himself, and life. He had kept her on a pedestal because it suited his need for security and self-esteem. While Tanya developed realistic caution. Tip changed from fear-driven behavior to nurturing. He could trust the discipline based on love rather than based on scare and rigidity. So he forgave and reconciled with Tanya.

Reconciliation is especially important in an ongoing relationship but keeping emotional and physical distance seems to work well enough in relationships where the people are going on their separate ways.

The more unfair and cruel the hurt, the worse the pain and anger. Also some people are far more sensitive than others. People with personality disorders feel more intensely about anything unfairly done to them although they themselves tend to be quite unfair. Some such people readily get enraged by minor rejections or innocent action taken as rejection. A strong need for forgiveness exists if hurt and anger linger, and it can be done in several stages.

Forgiveness can be done in the following stages:

- *Recognizing the wrong done to us.* It is useful to recognize the hurt in its depth. Like pulling out a weed with its roots, it is best to deal with the hurt in depth.
- *Experiencing the negative feelings.* These include hurt, anger, hate, rage, resentment, depression, fear, humiliation, jealousy, and insecurity.
- *Expressing feelings.* Feelings can be expressed in many ways: 1.) Talking out--verbalizing the feelings in the presence of an understanding person helps tremendously to relieve the negative feelings. If the listening person is the offender, it is even more beneficial. Talking out with a therapist enhances the healing. 2.) Writing out--writing about the various feelings also helps one to understand and ventilate the feelings. Some people find it useful to send the written material to the offender. In doing so, one has to consider the reactions of the offender. 3.) Acting-out symbolically-- expressing one's negative feelings in symbolic action such as tearing up the offender's picture.
- *Seeing the situation in perspective.* By seeing the hurt and anger in the larger perspective of our lives, we can gain useful understanding about ourselves, the other people involved and human nature.
- *Applying the spirit of the serenity prayer.* We can do this by taking two steps. One step is changing what can be changed for the better in ourselves and others. The second step is accepting what cannot realistically be changed.

Beyond the above stages of forgiveness, steps of reconciliation would include working in collaboration with the person who has hurt you. If that person is also willing to build a new relationship, then communicating the desire for reconciliation is an important preliminary step. With the goal of reconciliation in mind, the parties can share thoughts, feelings, and plans for the renewed relationship. In addition, the wrongdoer needs to express regret about the past offense and reassurance that it will not be repeated. Since actions speak louder than words, both regret and reassurance need to be backed by actions.

BENEFICIAL ROLES OF UNDERSTANDING AND COMPASSION

Understanding the reason for the wrongdoing of the victimizer can help a great deal in the process of forgiving and reconciling. I have seen this many times as adults who were abused as children learn that their abusers were abused too. This fact does not mean the abuse was excused, but it provides the larger perspective on human wrongs and tragedies. It also makes the victims feel good about themselves if they have not become abusers.

Sometimes the abuser may be a victim of an unfair social or cultural system. A Hindu man suffered from deep depression and anxiety partly because of rejection by his family for marrying a woman from a lower caste. He was bitter towards his family. He was a victim of the Hindu caste system, and he could not forgive his family until he recognized that they were also victims of the same caste system, which shaped their superegos and twisted their judgment. His family had also suffered much from the conflict.

Spirituality promotes forgiveness and reconciliation for several reasons. The open-mindedness gives them a larger perspective, including their own and other's strengths and weaknesses. The Christian prayer, the Lord's Prayer, for God's forgiveness of our trespasses as we forgive those who trespass against us indicates such insight. In many cases, I have been able to promote forgiveness by pointing out two matters to the victims of hurt: One, the victimizers were trying to meet their needs bypassing or going against their consciences; two, the victims too try to meet their own needs inconsistent with their consciences in some matters. To clarify, Amy had trouble forgiving her mother for her verbal abuse in the past since her mother never apologized. While her mother had used verbal abuse to relieve her tension, Amy was abusing alcohol for relief; while her mother did not apologize because of false pride, Amy was denying her alcohol abuse to keep her own false pride. Pointing these out to her helped Amy to forgive her mother.

Spiritually healthy people's good self-esteem and humility make it easier to give up negative feelings as a weapon to be used in hating others or oneself. Their ideals of forgiveness, compassion, love and their admiration for great historical figures who have shown these qualities equip them for forgiveness/reconciliation. Their belief in a spiritual realm and moral consequence of one's actions makes vengeance unnecessary. But justice with compassion is promoted for the common good. Spirituality promotes peace and goodness and enhances self-esteem of those trying to forgive and reconcile. Spiritual identity emphasizes our common humanity and consequently opposes the "us" against "them" mentality that promotes fear, mistrust, and hate.

Some people cause harm and break a relationship, and later when they feel like reconnecting, they expect to get back into the relationship without dealing with the past hurt. They take the attitude that the past is done with. That is unfair to the person who is left with the pain of the past hurt and the fear of its happening again. About a decade ago, Erma's daughter-in-law and son broke their relationship with her without explaining why they were doing so. Recently they started visiting Erma but would not talk about what caused the break off or the return. Although very pleased about their return, Erma was in much emotional turmoil, not knowing what happened so that she could really process it and put the past behind her. Erma had to deal with the situation in therapy and learn to accept her son and daughter-in-law with caution.

In another case, the person had to use a special technique to be able to forgive. Lynne had a strict superego and had made some progress in using her conscience better but some aspect of revenge was still important to her. She suffered for years from hurt and anger over her co-workers who made fun of her. She had felt so much pain that she had quit her job which she had liked in every other way. Even though she tried other jobs, she could not overcome her hurt and anger. She could not understand why her co-workers, most of them claiming to be Christians, hurt her. She felt that God had let her down and was equally surprised that God did not punish the evildoers who harmed her. An educational approach about human behavior, especially how the person who is different is often unfairly treated, helped Lynne somewhat. We also discussed how religious people may be guided by their superegos and not their consciences, and that helped her further. But she still felt that if people who harmed her had recognized their wrong and felt remorse, she could feel relieved. She imagined that her former co-workers felt proud of their victory and her defeat.

In order to help Lynne further, I tried a unique approach. After discussing the descriptions of near-death experiences, I asked her to imagine how her enemies would feel as they reviewed their lives in front of the Being of Light. Lynne imagined vividly how they regretted their actions. She felt relief as she imagined the remorse they would feel as they reviewed their wrongs in God's presence.

On a large scale, the Truth and Reconciliation Commission of South Africa headed by Nobel Laureate Bishop Desmond Tutu brought about forgiveness and reconciliation with former perpetrators of terrible offenses committed by many whites on blacks under the apartheid system. This approach was consistent with the African tradition of restorative justice which aims at healing the breach rather than simply punishing the criminal. The perpetrators had to confess publicly of the crimes they committed.

CONSCIENCE AND INTEGRATING THE PAST

All the benefits of understanding, compassion and spirituality in forgiveness and reconciliation noted above are the results of being guided by conscience. As we use our conscience, we forgive and reconcile with ourselves for the wrongs we do to us, using the steps of realistic guilt. Several features of conscience foster forgiveness and reconciliation; conscience promotes broad outlook and good reasoning instead of excessive feelings. So we can see the bitter fruits of keeping bitterness, judge what is useful for us and fair to others, and relieve ourselves from the burden of useless negative feelings, thoughts, and deeds. We do not deserve to turn the hurt caused by someone into our chronic pain. We can use our energies for better purposes.

Conscience promotes transformation for a better future rather than revenge. So it makes use of opportunities for reconciliation. If the other person also uses conscience then reconciliation is easy because that person will show regret and would reassure that he or she will prevent repetition of the hurt. Conscientious people also tend to provide opportunity and encouragement to others to forgive and reconcile. If reconciliation is not possible, the better choice is letting the hard feelings go while keeping a safe distance from the victimizer. A superego that is conditioned to hold grudges can prevent forgiveness and reconciliation.

Integrating the past involves forgiveness, reconciliation, letting harmful feelings go, and learning what is useful from our experiences, all of which help rather than hinder us in fulfilling our hearts and souls.

10. HAVE A BALANCED PRESENT AND FUTURE

"The unaware life is a mechanical life. It's not human, it's programmed, conditioned. We may as well be a stone, a block of wood."[41]

Anthony de Mello

"If it were not for hope, the heart would break."

A proverb

The present or current time is indeed a wonderful present or gift which presents us with multiple choices in dealing with the now as well as the past and the future. Our biggest power and greatest blessing lies in making right choices in the present. It can also turn out to be a big curse if we crucify ourselves in the present, as someone observed, between the two thieves--unhealthy guilt from the past and worries about the future. Just as we do when we walk, it is important to utilize the healthy momentum from the past, maintain balance in the present and proceed harmoniously into the future in our journey of life. If excessive attachments to the past pull our legs or if we push too hard to grab something in the future--in either case, if we offset the present balance--we fall flat on our face. Of course that might prompt us to look up and see a larger horizon. Hope plays an important role in our present balance and future direction.

HOPE

Hope is a powerful common ground between psychiatry and religion. St. Paul emphasized faith, hope and love. While religions differ in many ways, they all provide hope of happiness here and hereafter for their followers. Somewhat similarly, although various forms of psychological therapies differ in their theories and techniques, all of them provide hope of improvement for the patient. Eminent psychiatrist Jerome Frank has found in his research that hope is a significant common factor that helps patients utilizing different psychological therapies.

While hope is therapeutic, hopelessness is an indicator of high suicide risk. In the Greek tragedy *Antigone* by Sophocles, King Creon punishes Antigone by sending her to a cave for an act of disobedience. Creon does not listen to his son Heamon's pleas to release Antigone who is the love of his life. But the King listens to the prophet Tiresias and decides to free Antigone. By then she had already committed suicide and Heamon too takes his own life. If only Antigone had been hopeful and waited for some more time, both the tragic deaths could have been prevented, and their story could have ended happily.

Hopelessness is often based on a faulty way of thinking--by a narrowed perspective. Often those who commit suicide tend to think that, if they cannot have a particular mate or a specific job or something else that is very important to them, then life is not worth living. Take the case of a bright, hardworking and ambitious young man. He was very good in flying airplanes and had set his highest goal to become a fighter pilot in the Air Force. But, unfortunately, the Air Force rejected him because his height did not match official specifications. In his frustration, he committed suicide. He could have been an excellent commercial pilot or done well in many other ways. Sadly, he had narrowed his options to being a fighter pilot or nothing. A narrow either/or mentality is not healthy in any circumstances, and it is a deadly serious problem when it involves a life or death decision. On numerous occasions I have discussed this point with people who have attempted suicide, and they have found it very useful.

Hope affects our perception, thinking, feeling and actions positively. Hope involves seeing useful options to pursue. It may be a dim vision many times, but the hopeful person pursues the lead. The urgency of a situation makes us look keenly and pursue vigorously various possibilities. This is the secret behind the time-honored observation that "necessity is the mother of invention." Hope stimulates our imagination and motivation to achieve our goals and helps to tune out discouraging thoughts and feelings.

Hope is not unrealistic optimism or rigid expectation. Realism and flexibility accompany healthy hope, and the hopeful person does not get too frustrated if things do not work out as hoped. Such realism reduces the frustration from failed expectations and helps to keep hope alive.

Anticipating and planning for predictable future events is obviously healthy. It reduces stress, deepens a sense of our participation in the processes and rhythms of life, and stimulates creative imagination. Anticipation and planning for the significant passages of life are especially important. Flexibility to modify our plans to suit changes in our situation is equally important. In several sad cases of failed marriages I have dealt with, one of the partners had wanted to back out some weeks or days before the wedding but did not because the ceremony was already arranged. Such rigidity, especially in crucial matters, is self-defeating.

Unlike anticipation and planning, worrying is not productive; it is really like a car stuck in the mud spinning wheels and stirring up mud. Anxious individuals tend to worry; and it keeps their anxiety levels high. Learning to let go of useless feelings and relax helps to alleviate this problem. One complication with worrying is that it takes away from sufficient focus on the present moment and useful visions for the future.

VISION--CREATIVE IMAGINATION ABOUT THE FUTURE

As Proverbs 19: 18 teaches, "Where there is no vision, the people perish." One quality of great leaders is a vision for the future of their people, involving creative imagination with hope and wishes for a good future. The many blessings of freedom and democracy we enjoy today are the results of creative visions of many great leaders.

Creative imagination about the future is very useful to generate energy and enthusiasm to move forward. But a vision can turn into a nightmare if it becomes a rigid expectation which fails to materialize, as in the case of the young pilot who committed suicide. Let the imagination motivate pursuing good choices with reasonable flexibility.

It is important for us to have long term and short term goals. A sense of a calling or a particular mission in life can be a powerful force that can organize our energies and give special meaning to life. Even those who do not have an extraordinary mission can aim for self-actualization or fulfillment of their abilities within their limits. What is useful is to give enough time and energy to our more important goals. I recall reading Goethe's advice that things that matter most must never be at the mercy of things which matter least. Along with doing our daily duties, we need to pursue our long-term goals to make our lives more fulfilling. Taking a few minutes every day to reflect on how we are progressing in achieving our goals can be especially useful. It is also useful to avoid excessive distraction by the mass media, gossips, petty conflicts, and temptations.

Some people have a distant vision but no imagination about the steps towards the goal. Rick had been withdrawn socially for many years, but he had a distant vision of working as a missionary because he had considerable knowledge about religion. He talked about this goal but refused to consider any steps towards achieving the goal. Refusing even to consider getting active in his church, he used his distant goal as an excuse for not making immediate choices and acting on them.

MAKE CHOICES AND ACT

We can be unbalanced or paralyzed at present by being pulled by different wishes and wants related to different needs and external circumstances, as well as the guidance of superego and conscience. The more we can be aware of how these conflicting factors affect our lives now and are likely to affect us in the future, we can use our consciences to make reasonable choices. Emotional and spiritual sufferings and tensions can be examined to understand conflicts. When strong feelings are involved, reducing the feelings by calming thoughts or talking with a helpful person is quite useful. Information and opinion from experts may be needed in deciding complex issues.

After deciding on our choices, we have to use the powers of our will and imagination to carry out our choices. Practice of mindfulness meditation (see details in Appendix) is particularly useful for both increasing awareness and disciplining the mind and body. Just paying more attention to thoughts and feelings can help to enhance our awareness. Merely labeling inaction as laziness won't help because it doesn't promote progress, and it lowers self-esteem.

When a patient told me he was just lazy, we explored   what needs he was meeting by being lazy. He was meeting his need for pleasure by enjoying watching television and eating, and meeting his need for comfort by avoiding the stresses of work and love. Then we found ways for him to have better comfort and pleasure without excessive stress by gradually expanding his life in social and spiritual areas. And he made much progress.

In order to make the best of the present and future, we have to have good awareness and focus.

AWARENESS AND FOCUS

I know two people, Fran and Frank, who have opposite problems. Frank is too focused on his goal and has poor awareness of other things going on in and around him. He tends to stumble on toys, books, or any objects on the floor or hit his leg on the coffee table if it is a little misplaced. He also has a hard time letting go of hurt feelings. And he frequently irritates his wife by repeating himself if he is uptight about something. Fran, on the other hand, is too little focused. She is so aware of everything around her that she would straighten many of the misplaced things on her way to get something from another room. So much so, her main tasks get delayed and sometimes even forgotten. Her poor focus frustrates her spouse.

Exercises which focus on one thing and let distractions go strengthen our ability to focus. An example of this is concentration meditation focused on breathing or on a sacred word. Mindfulness meditations where the person calmly observes thoughts and feelings increases awareness.

We have to focus our attention on particular tasks often, but keep a broad awareness too. A deeper level of awareness--an understanding of the important issues of life and death--provides the foundation for making crucial choices because we want our choices to promote our ultimate meaning. The Hindu scripture Gita illustrates this point brilliantly. The hero Arjuna is a man of action, an excellent archer and great warrior. Once his great archery trainer Drona tested the skills of his large number of students. He told them one by one to be ready to shoot an artificial bird placed on top of a tree. Drona asked what the students saw. Every student except Arjuna said that he saw Drona, the other students, the tree and the bird, but Arjuna said that he saw only the bird's head. Then Drona ordered Arjuna to shoot, and he instantly shot off the bird's head. Such was Arjuna's capacity to focus and act.

Later in life, Arjuna had to fight on the side of his brothers (Pandavas) against his cousins. Pandavas had a very just cause to fight for the kingdom that rightfully belonged to them. Their cousins had deceptively taken over the kingdom and rejected Pandavas' offer to settle even for five small plots of land. So, they had to fight; but when the time came for Arjuna to start fighting, he was paralyzed by despair about injuring his own relatives. In effect, his greatest skill was useless at the very time when it was most needed. Arjuna had chosen Lord Krishna, an incarnation of God, as his charioteer and advisor. Krishna discussed with Arjuna the issues of life and death, passion and suffering, devotion and duty. Arjuna received a broad vision about life and death from Krishna. With this deep awareness, he overcame his doubts and despair and valiantly and unselfishly performed his duty with devotion to God.

Interestingly, Arjuna, the master of focused action, took the time to gain deep awareness to choose the right course of action. This approach is in sharp contrast to the quick fixes, one minute solutions, and fast actions based on superficial views that have become fashionable for many people. Matters of social and spiritual values and the meaning of life are essential parts of deep awareness.

How the broad picture of life changes people's choices was shown when seven hundred couples in Houston, Texas, withdrew their divorce petitions after the terrible terrorist attack on America on September 11, 2001.

DEATH AWARENESS

Many great thinkers have observed that the awareness of our mortality vastly enriches our lives. Yet blocking out the awareness of death is common and often the unfortunate result is superficiality in the understanding of and involvement in life. People who are dealing with terminal cancer often show significant personal growth from their awareness and acceptance of death. They show more love and understanding of themselves, others, the world, and God. They become less defensive and fearful and enjoy the beauty of nature and the simple pleasures of life.

Dixon, a severely depressed patient, was very difficult to treat because of his negative attitude about life and about treatment. Although medications helped him to an extent, he continued to focus on everything negative and think of suicide. He refused hospitalization even when his depression got worse. His wife kept a close watch, but one day he sneaked out of the house and made a serious suicide attempt. As he recovered from his injuries, he changed. He became open to life's blessings including love and goodness, and his rigidity, pessimistic views, and arrogance were gone. With these changes, his depression improved rapidly.

Spirituality helps us to be aware of our mortality in the larger context of the eternal and the infinite, and such a view markedly diminishes death anxiety and ennobles life. The anxiety about death, the strongest of all anxieties, is part of many anxiety disorders. John, a patient with serious hypochondriasis, stayed in bed for many days, ate only meager food and constantly worried about his health. He had no significant physical illness, just minor stomach troubles. His real problem was excessive fear of death which tended to become intense when he was under much stress. With much coaxing, I got him to write his obituary and talk about his imagination of his death and thus confront his fear of death. He was persuaded to read Tolstoy's story *The Death of Ivan Illyich;* when he read about Ivan's sickness, John got scared, but he felt relief when he read about Ivan's change from a selfish and superficial man to a compassionate and deeper person as he faced his death. Reading about the healthy personality transformation of people who had Near Death Experiences further relieved his excessive fear of death and enabled him to focus on fulfilling his life.

Spiritual exercises may increase or decrease our awareness, depending on how the practitioner uses the exercises. Reading scripture, prayer, listening to spiritual teachings, and the like can increase our awareness and increase our love and wisdom. In contrast, spiritual exercises can also work like lullabies, decreasing people's awareness and reinforcing fanatical views that go against love and wisdom. Joe's case illustrates the effect of the fanatical side of religion.

Joe, a conscientious, compassionate, and spiritual person, had done fairly well despite his serious mental illness. Usually, he had good awareness of his strengths and weakness and kept his stress level low. However, when he got involved with religious fanatics who read scriptures and prayed a lot but remained superficial and hateful towards people who are different, he lost his healthy awareness and hated himself for his limitations. Soon he became agitated and psychotic. As I pointed out to him this pattern, he distanced from fanatic groups.

While a deep awareness and a useful focus help to maintain balance, many people suffer from the inability to let go of a focus when it is no longer useful.

PROBLEM IN LETTING GO OF A FOCUS

If we hold on to a focus when it serves no useful purpose, we waste our energies and diminish our overall awareness. And the things that we get hung up on usually keep harmful feelings stirred up. An example of this problem is the case of a bright, hard working, dependable, loving, and fairly good-looking young man who had a major weakness. He used to go to pieces if a girl rejected him. Several times he became severely depressed as his mind focused on the rejection. He made significant progress when he developed good capacity to shift focus to what is useful for him and keep a broader awareness of life and love.

Excessive focusing on a hurtful incident often makes forgiveness very difficult. Often a lack of broader awareness is the cause of excessive and narrow focusing.

Many people continue to suffer by holding on to anger or grief because of distorted ideas such as the notion that one should not forgive but get even, and the impression that one cannot stop grieving a serious loss. A broader perspective helps to overcome such misconceptions.

The Three H's That Help to Keep Our Vision Clear

Humility, honesty, and humor help us tremendously to keep a clear view of the present and future. Arrogant people are likely to twist reality to maintain their false but proud image. But the humble person does not carry such burden, and enjoys the freedom of honesty.

Authenticity and respect for truthfulness are strong forces that help us to keep a clear vision. People who genuinely respect truth try hard to see the reality and feel good about seeking truth. While it is good for us to see the reality, it is equally important to recognize that many people prefer to live in a dream world than to be awake and alert to the larger realities of life.

An intelligent, middle-aged lady worked hard to impart good knowledge and insight to a group of people. She was really trying to help them in their expressed goal of spiritual growth. In reality, though, they were resistant to growth. In fact, when she pushed them a little to open their eyes to deeper understanding, they became resentful and angry. The lady was frustrated. I posed her a question: "Could it be that they really want to sleep, and you are trying to wake them up?" After a brief reflection she said: "Yes. That is it. I should let sleeping dogs lie." I added, "Some people prefer to lie to themselves." We both laughed.

Humor involves looking at a situation with gentleness, intellectual pleasure, and a level of acceptance. The acceptance is not that the action is perfect but that the imperfection is not terrible. It does not take away from the motivation to change for the better. Humor can reduce the stress from self-rejection and prevent self-hate. Like swallowing a sugarcoated bitter pill, we can view many unpleasant but important matters with a sense of humor rather than block off with denial or remain frustrated.

Some Causes For Poor Awareness

- excessive feelings that focus our attention on one thing and reduce our overall awareness
- lack of sufficient feelings to alert us
- wrong ideas that distort our view
- false pride in a particular theory or world view
- excessive psychological and spiritual defenses
- excessive attachment or aversion to something

Jesus taught us to remove the blinders that block our vision and enjoy the freedom of truth. Proverbs teach us that the heart of the prudent gets knowledge and the ear of the wise seeks knowledge. Our awareness increases with wisdom and with love. One of the greatest benefits of genuine love is that far from being blind, it broadens and sharpens our vision through better understanding.

An important aspect of our awareness is our identity, and a balanced identity also prevents us from distorting reality to maintain a false identity. Healthy awareness and focus enable us to enjoy the present and to preserve balance as we move on. The Buddha told a story about enjoying the present even in a crisis. A man was out in the field when he noticed a tiger. The tiger chased him as he ran for his life. The man reached a precipice. There he stumbled and started falling. But he caught a bush growing by the side of the precipice. As he clung there suspended between the deep chasm below and the tiger hunting him above, he saw a nice ripe fruit growing on the bush. Holding on to the bush with one hand, he plucked the fruit with his other hand and enjoyed eating it. That poor fellow found himself in an extreme situation but still had the presence of mind to enjoy the present as much as he could. Often, when we are faced with even far less difficult situations, we get so focused on problems that we miss valuable chances for enjoyment and enlightenment.

PRIORITIZE AND LIMIT JUGGLING

At any given moment, we are usually juggling many matters related to past, present, and future and faced with choices based on our needs, circumstances, external demands and guidance of superego and conscience. Even the best juggler in a circus can juggle only a limited number of objects properly. We have to limit how many matters we juggle with and we have to prioritize our choices so that we do not ignore the truly important matters.

If we look at the overall picture of life, we can realize that there is no use including in our present juggling thoughts or feelings about numerous insignificant matters. Practices such as meditation and centering prayer help to calm the mind and make it easier to prevent useless or harmful matters intruding into our mind and distracting us from our priorities. Understanding of our needs, circumstances, and inner guides sharpens our awareness of the forces we are handling in making choices.

CONSCIENCE AND PRESENT BALANCE AND FUTURE DIRECTION

Conscience helps with present balance and future direction by guiding us to choose what is good at present and what is good for the future. As we saw in the previous chapter, conscience helps to cut off the strings from the past that cause unhealthy pull on us. Conscience helps limit and prioritize the number of choices we juggle at present. As for future direction, conscience guides us to make choices that are conducive to promote psychological and spiritual fulfillment.

Fortunately conscience is not picky and punitive like a rigid superego nor does it downplay important matters like a loose superego, and it gives us enough leeway for human follies and foibles. Conscience helps us to get rid of negative feelings from the past by forgiveness, reconciliation, and acceptance of unchangeable realities. The feeling of guilt, shame, and anger coming from our conscience motivates us to make healthy changes.

Since conscience uses compassion and love, we can really be straight with our conscience regarding our wrongs while it is too painful and scary to do so with a strict superego. But it is tempting to pick up spiritual defenses from our social groups and we have to prevent this problem.

Awareness and conscience go hand in hand. With increased awareness, conscience has better data on which to base its decision and function more efficiently. And conscience prompts us to keep a broader and deeper awareness of life. Spiritually healthy people are open to improve their awareness, but extremists resist it.

Conscience helps future direction by providing healthy guidelines and using the wisdom from past experiences and other sources to do what is healthy. It is helpful in many situations to focus on one day at a time to prevent being overwhelmed by big tasks, but we also need a sense of overall direction and a feeling of hope for the future. On numerous occasions I have utilized the story of psychiatrist and author Viktor Frankl's survival in concentration camps and similar examples to build hope, courage, meaning, and a sense of direction. Certainly, one key to fulfillment is steering life in a healthy direction, not letting it drift.

11. ENJOY COMFORT AND PLEASURE

"In short, the healthiest people seem to be pleasure loving, pleasure seeking, pleasure creating individuals."[42]

Robert Ornstein and Daniel Sobel

A psychologically and spiritually fulfilling life involves comfort and healthy pleasures including spiritual joy. Many people mistakenly think spirituality is opposed to pleasure more or less, a misunderstanding largely due to ascetic and masochistic strains in religions which have caused, and still cause, much unhappiness to many people. With the impact of consumerism and hedonism and with better psychological understanding of our human needs, many religious and social groups accept the importance of healthy pleasures, but still plenty of confusion persists. And spiritual joy deserves far more than the extremely low attention it usually gets.

COMFORT

Discomforts from unpleasant feelings, often caused by unmet or wrongly met needs, are common causes for the lack of fulfillment which may produce symptoms of stress: tension, irritability, frustration, sleep disturbance, decreased or increased appetite, tiredness, and sexual dysfunction. Many women say they become "mean bitches" and many men admit they act like a "horse's rear end" if their needs for affection and sex are not met. Unmet needs for sleep can even cause psychosis. Unmet needs for security and esteem lead many people to do wild and crazy things to gain power and recognition. Many youths join gangs to relieve isolation and boredom while many adults join cults and fanatic groups to enjoy the comforts of believing and belonging. It is extremely useful to recognize the particular need behind one's distress and healthy ways to meet that need.

If the discomfort is strong, then the temptation to find relief by *any means* is strong too. Many times it is after falling for the temptation and feeling guilty that we focus on the problem. Such was the case with Willie, a spiritually oriented man, who did not think about the distress from unmet needs and temptation for unhealthy release building up. He had a tendency, at times, to work excessively and spend too little time in relaxing and pleasurable activities such as playing musical instruments and having good times with friends. He was single and occasionally engaged in casual sex with strangers quite contrary to his principles. He felt guilty after these sexual encounters and was afraid of scandal, but these negative feelings did not stop his behavior. So he sought therapy, and as we analyzed the situation, it became clear that Willie engaged in casual sex after a period of starving himself of enough relaxation and healthy pleasures. With this insight, he practiced relaxation and had enough healthy pleasures regularly. He overcame his sexual indiscretion and grew psychologically and spiritually by understanding human needs and using conscience well. His enlightenment enabled him to help many others to do the same.

In order to relieve intense feelings, we tend to do many things hastily and act against our own better judgment. People hastily quit jobs, marry, divorce, act violently, and ironically, even attempt suicide to relieve intense fear of death. Many people are impulsive because they have much difficulty in delaying or denying their strong desires. Addicts have much problem in saying "no" to their craving for their object of addiction.

Manipulative people exploit others by stimulating in them strong feelings of guilt, shame, anger, fear, lust, greed, craving for power or pleasure and the like. Once the strong feeling is stimulated, the manipulator offers something to relieve the feeling in return for what the manipulator demands. This is like muddying waters and then fishing in it. If you make a mistake under the pressure or persuasion by such people, they further use that mistake against you. One has to be cautious to prevent being victimized by such villains.

It is important to recognize our uncomfortable thoughts and feelings. Then we can judge what is causing these feelings. Based on that judgment, we can take further useful steps, whether it is to let the feelings go or pursue actions to handle certain needs behind the discomfort. Methods of calming feelings and using discipline help to counteract excessive feelings and impulsiveness.

PLEASURE

Both in the West and in the East there have been opposing tendencies--one accepting and supporting the importance of pleasures and another rejecting and denigrating pleasures. The Greek philosophers in general considered pleasure an important part of life. The Roman rulers had the good sense to provide the public both bread and circus. But the Stoics ("stoic" means passionless), especially in first and second centuries A. D., rejected pleasure. The anti-pleasure views of the Stoics influenced Christianity. This is unfortunate because Jesus feasted many times, unlike John the Baptizer who led a stoic life.

Kama Sutra, the first book on sexology and marital life, by the Hindu sage Vatsyayana written around fourth century, A. D., describes various ways to enjoy sexual and sensual pleasures. In spite of such teachings, anti-pleasure and even masochistic trends have also existed in Hinduism.

Vatsyayana himself raised many objections to pleasure: pleasure seeking can lead to distress, loss of respect from others, and to contacts with people of low character; temptations of pleasure can lead to impurity, sinful acts, and produce carelessness, laziness and disregard for the future. Interestingly, we can hear such objections to pleasure even today. After listing the objections, Vatsyayana dismissed them, asserting that pleasures are as necessary for our well-being as food. He, however, advocated the pursuit of pleasure with moderation, caution, and consideration of others. Interestingly, Aristotle had also considered pleasure essential for life and staunchly promoted the idea of moderation. Vatsyayana concluded that those who pursue ethical living along with wealth and pleasure would enjoy happiness both in life here and hereafter. If we examine the benefits of pleasure, we can appreciate his wisdom.

BENEFITS OF PLEASURE

- relieves tension and stress, and relaxes
- makes us feel good
- reinforces the activities that are pleasurable
- strengthens our bonds by giving pleasure to others and allowing others to please us
- enlivens us physically and mentally
- spiritual pleasures reinforce spiritual as well as psychological and physical well-being
- pleasure prevents or reduces boredom, frustration, and apathy
- increases interest and motivation
- strengthens or supports willpower
- stimulates imagination
- healthy pleasures can eliminate the need for unhealthy excitement and stimulation
- Often pleasure signals what is nourishing to us
  As we satisfy various human needs we experience comfort and pleasure. The stronger the need, the more intense the pleasure of fulfilling that need.

Pleasure is a wonderful part of our bonding with others. As we enjoy giving pleasure to those we love and accepting pleasure from them our bonds are strengthened. One of the most pleasurable aspects of child-rearing is the vicarious delight in the child's enjoyment. Close relationships, especially friendships, involve sharing comfort and pleasure. It may be in joking, teasing, playing cards, or engaging in games, intellectual discussions, sharing meals, watching movies, visiting places, and so on. Lovers thrive on exchanging pleasures of various kinds including sensuous and sexual enjoyment. Variety and novelty are very useful in enhancing pleasure. Likewise long duration of the pleasurable activity may be desirable; however, usually, the pleasure has to be of low intensity to be enjoyed for a long time.

Sharing pleasures helps tremendously to relieve frustrations, stresses, and pains that occur in relationships, especially in close relationships. Many couples make love as part of making up after fights.

In *Healthy Pleasures* Robert Ornstein and David Sobel talk about an "F Index": the frequency of fornication minus the frequency of fights. Happiness in marriage coincides with high "F Index." If a couple fights 12 times a month but has sex 16 times, their "F Index" is +4. My clinical experience is somewhat different. While a good sex life is very useful for a happy marriage, frequent sex does not seem to compensate for serious marital conflicts. One divorced woman told me: "We connected very well at our tail ends but we couldn't connect at our head ends, and so we split." Undoubtedly, couples who have much fun together can withstand many conflicts, and their lives are individually and collectively enriched. Shared healthy pleasures create strong bonds among family members.

Problems With Pleasure

While healthy pleasure is a great virtue, addictions and anhedonia or lack of pleasure are vices or serious problems. Addictions are characterized by lack of control over the habit, imbalance as well as persistence of the behavior in spite of negative consequences. The negative consequences include problems in health, family life, finances, and work. Various addictions are pleasure seeking gone astray. An essential part of any addiction is the pleasurable state of feeling "high." When they stop the addiction, they go through withdrawal symptoms which cause different levels of suffering depending on the type and depth of addiction. Addicts are so compelled by the need to experience this "high" and the aversion to face the distress of withdrawal that they lose balance and self-control over the addictive substance or relationship. Therefore, harmful consequences often do not stop their addictive behavior.

The opposite extreme of addiction is rejection of pleasure which is often caused by excessive fear of losing control, fear of punishment from God, ignorance, fear of rejection by authorities or others, and perverse pride in a stoic lifestyle. Rejection of pleasures can make people apathetic, frustrated, cynical, cold, callous, judgmental, narrow-minded, sadistic, masochistic, selfish, and mean. These people's energies are often channeled into being too defensive, controlling and distressing others. The Taliban rulers of Afghanistan prohibited entertainments such as music, movies, and flying kites but they seemed to enjoy beating women for not covering themselves completely and watching public executions.

Some people claim: "If you are not busy working, you are lazy." Brian was too focused on work and learned the importance of pleasure the hard way. He was a hard working, honest, responsible, intense person with a hot temper which he kept in control most of the time, but used to "mouth off a bit" when he lost his cool. He had built up a successful business, but the stress of keeping it up was high. His wife was helping him with the business too. For several months before getting therapy, Brian lost his temper increasingly often and took his frustration out on his wife. He was stressed out with work, and he did not take time to relax and enjoy. Growing increasingly frustrated by his behavior, his wife urged him to seek help. By then he was anxious and depressed. Medications for anxiety and depression helped him to some extent, but he made significant progress only when he cut down his work stress and found time to exercise, relax, and have fun with his family. Had he not made these changes to meet his and his wife's need for comfort and pleasure, his wife would have left him, and he would have lost a great deal financially.

Two types of pleasures deserve our special attention here. They are spiritual joy and good humor.

SPIRITUAL PLEASURES (JOYS)

Spiritual joys can be of various types, such as pleasure gained from promotion of goodness, cultivation of wisdom, spiritual exercises, ethical living, and spiritual experiences. These activities may involve enormous struggle, energy expenditure, and sacrifice of certain other pleasurable activities. As we empathize with a man who is seriously sick, and as we bear the stress of helping him beyond any personal obligation, we can also experience a sense of peace and a good feeling deep down about our own action under the circumstance. Those positive feelings in doing good are part of spiritual joy.

Sharing one's spiritual joy with someone who can really appreciate the experience is both emotionally and spiritually pleasing. I recall the joy of a patient and her delight in sharing her experience several months after discharge from the hospital. When she was hospitalized for depression and drug abuse, she was quite difficult and manipulative. I had explained to her how she could use her conscience to guide her choices and, thus, transform her personality disorder and turn her life around. Although she had had psychiatric treatments previously, her personality disorder had not been dealt with. She had cleverly hid her pattern of maladaptive choices, but her life had already become complicated by her personality disorder and drug abuse. She was single and had financial and legal problems as well as difficulty finding a regular job. She, however, followed my recommendations, continued in therapy, stayed drug free and found a lower paying job while working towards a much better career. Although she was struggling with these stresses and had no dates (she could not stand not having a man in her life previously), she experienced inner peace and spiritual joy since she was living by her conscience. She beamed with delight as she shared her joy with me.

GOOD SENSE OF HUMOR

A good sense of humor is very healthy both psychologically and spiritually. The Bible teaches: "A merry heart doeth good like a medicine" (Proverbs 17:22). Humor helps us to stand back and take a gentle and creative look at a situation, especially a difficult problem. Some of the benefits of laughter are that it

- brightens mood
- relieves or reduces pain
- gives exercise to muscles of the face, abdomen, diaphragm, and shoulders
- releases tensions
- removes pretensions and masks to varying degrees
- improves the immune system
- improves relationships when fun is shared
- reduces fear and hate
- gets the other person to lower defenses and view problems more realistically.

Truly spiritual people generally have a good sense of humor about life and about themselves. Look, for instance, at the sixteenth-century Indian emperor Akbar, probably the greatest Moslem ruler in history, who is famous for his spirituality. Once Akbar asked his bright minister Birbal to find and bring to the court the three greatest fools in the country. After a month, Birbal returned to the court with only one man. Birbal explained to Akbar the reason this man was one of the three greatest fools: he was riding a donkey and carrying a heavy load on his shoulder to lighten the burden for the animal. Akbar inquired about the other two fools. Birbal claimed himself as the second greatest fool for accepting the assignment to look for fools. As to the third greatest fool, Birbal pointed to the emperor himself for sending someone on such a foolish quest. The palace resounded with everyone's laughter.

How to Strengthen Your Funny Bone

- Learn from the masters. Dip into the rich reservoirs of jokes, humorous stories, funny anecdotes, and the like. Notice how such stories, incidents, and even clever one-liners use interesting combinations of words and ideas in ways that are amusing and often meaningful. Loosen up your psychological and spiritual defenses, excessive fears, and rigidities.
- You might memorize some humorous punch-lines and interesting stories. As you use them in appropriate situations, you are likely to get your own humorous ideas on other

occasions.

- You can exaggerate your feelings in a humorous way. Dramatize for fun, not for acting out in anger or fear.
- Keep an eye on the funny ironies of life, like observing the boomerang that misses the target and returns to you.
- Along with eating, exercise, and keeping up personal hygiene, make it a daily habit to exercise your funny bone. Keep some good jokes in store for handy use when fresh supply is not available.
- Using your conscience instead of a strict superego is very useful to strengthen your humor.
- Look at cartoons in newspapers and humorous stories in magazines. View the news with a touch of irony and wit.

In your practice of daily reflection, be sure to include a sense of humor. Consider whether you are getting your recommended daily allowance of humor. When your sunny side is up, make much hay of humor so you can use it when you go haywire during the rainy days of life.

SPIRITUALITY AND PLEASURE

Pleasure and healthy spirituality go hand in hand in two ways. Spiritually healthy people enjoy pleasures in moderation, and spirituality is extremely beneficial in dealing with unhealthy pleasures, especially addictions.

A spiritually-oriented friend confessed to me once that his traditionally-minded physician wife enjoyed sex, but she thought that truly spiritual people would enjoy celibacy, not sex. Many strictly religious people are filled with fear, shame, guilt, self-hate and the like, in regard to their passions, pleasures and enjoyments even though they are not doing anything harmful or unfair. They live rigid, boring, even masochistic lives, missing healthy pleasures. Often they are frustrated, resentful, apathetic, or hateful towards others; so their relationships suffer tremendously. Therefore, naturally, they tend to resent other people having fun and try to impose their rigidities on others.

The idea that spiritual people are boring and bored morons constantly worrying about doing right, taking everything too seriously, and waiting to die and get over this "vale of sorrow" is false. There are people who fit such descriptions, but their spirituality is too harsh, and not worth emulating. St. Theresa once remarked that, "A saint sad is a sad saint" and prayed to God to deliver her from "sour-faced saints." Besides other healthy pleasures, the spiritual person can enjoy spiritual joy.

When we positively promote goodness there is a deep inner joy even though we may be physically and emotionally stressed by the work. This joy is something we deserve, and it will help us to pursue spiritually healthy living in spite of various difficulties in doing so. Some spiritual people get confused about such delight and try to reject it or suppress it because they think that they are only doing their duty. And many people seem to miss spiritual joy because it is often subtle, compared to physical pleasures. It is important to savor and tune up spiritual joy because it strengthens us emotionally and spiritually rather than make us conceited or superficial.

In the book of Genesis Chapter 1 the statement, "and God saw that it was good," occurs five times and finally in verse 3 it is stated, "God saw everything He made and it was very good." These verses show God's enjoyment of creation.

Vocal and instrumental music, dances of various kinds, feasts, beautiful decorations, fireworks and the like connected with religious services and celebrations combine sensual delights with spirituality and enhance people's overall fulfillment. In many parts of the world, it is not unusual for people of different faiths who do not worship together to join in and enjoy festivals of other religions. Such partying together reinforces our common humanity. In many instances religious extremists have objected their members participating in the ceremonies of another religion.

In Hinduism God is called "Satchitananda" meaning truth, consciousness, and bliss. Mother Teresa, one of the most experienced people in dealing with the poor, has observed many times the clean, clear joy of the poor people in the simple everyday blessings of life and their happiness with their families. Meister Eckhart, a great mystic of the 14th century, preached about the joy and happiness of acts of justice and compassion. Also according to Eckhart, God laughs and plays over good deeds. Thomas Merton, a Catholic monk and author, was known for his joy. In fact, a friend of Merton stated: "He was before and above all a man of great joy, joy in God, joy in his friends and companions, joy in all God's creation."[43] The Dalai Lama is popular partly because of his good humor.

Creation as God's play is a prominent theme in Hinduism. Even for many religious people, who would hold their breath of pleasure until they reach heaven, the hope of everlasting joy thereafter is extremely important. The hope of heaven with all its pleasures is as much or more powerful a motivator as the fear of hell for the believers.

The success of the spiritually oriented twelve step programs in the treatment of addictions is not surprising because addictions are spiritual as well as physical and psychological problems. Addicts increasingly get away from a spiritual way of living into unethical lifestyles. They lie, cheat, steal, harm their own and other people's health and well-being, shirk responsibility, and have no realistic guilt. As the addiction gets worse the spiritual decline becomes increasingly severe. While we still cannot alter the genes that play their role in addictions, we can alter the psychological and spiritual factors, and spirituality is the most powerful tool at our disposal for transformation.

The results of dealing with addictions were very disappointing until the twelve step programs became an integral part of the treatment. Numerous patients I have treated for addictions have told me later how much more enjoyable and pleasant their lives had become as they replaced the "highs" of addiction with healthy pleasures, especially the peace and joy of ethical living--practicing love and wisdom. In order to overcome addiction, addicts have to face their powerlessness over the addiction instead of using denial and lies. Reliance on a Higher Power is very helpful. Group support, prayer, meditation, constant vigilance, altruistic action, and healthy pleasures are, likewise, of great importance.

Conscience, Comfort, and Pleasure

Living by conscience involves self-discipline to face discomfort and do what is useful and fair in spite of negative feelings caused by our own desires or other people's behavior. People of conscience have empathy and compassion for other people's suffering, and sense of responsibility for their own actions. Addicts, however, use spiritual defenses and continue their destructive behavior. Many wives complain about their husbands' addiction to watching games and men complain about women's excessive shopping. If people use their conscience and examine such complaints, they would make good changes.

As the Islamic mystic Rumi had taught, one kind of delight can be replaced by a better delight. This is especially applicable to addicts. The better delight can be a combination of healthy pleasures.

With a realistic understanding of the importance of comfort and pleasure, we can use the guidance of our consciences and find healthy ways to fulfill these needs.

12. SATISFY SEXUALITY

"The husband should give to his wife her conjugal rights and likewise the wife to her husband."

St. Paul, 1 Corinthians 7:3

"Thus if men and women act according to each others' liking, their love for each other will not be lessened even in one hundred years."

Vatsyayana in *Kama Sutra*

Sexuality is a prime example of a wonderful gift which we can use very beneficially, use hardly at all or abuse in many ways. A study published in the *Journal of American Medical Association* in February 1999, estimated that 43% of women and 31% of men in the U.S. have sexual dysfunction like low sexual desire, lack of orgasm, erectile dysfunction and premature ejaculation. Reportedly, only less than 10% of people with sexual dysfunction seek treatment. Twelve million new cases of sexually transmitted diseases, including genital herpes and AIDS, are estimated to occur in the U. S. alone annually. Add to it millions of unwanted pregnancies, half a million women dying in childbirth globally a year, sexual abuses and so on. All these cry out for conscientious use of sexuality to promote its great benefits and to prevent its tragic misuses and abuses.

Religions give tremendous importance to sexuality. *Religions can rightfully tell their members to obey their rules to gain the benefits the religions offer; so people ought to take the teachings of their religion seriously.*

Incidentally, I will be making several references to the Catholic Church in this chapter because it is the largest religious group both in the U.S. and in the world, and it has taken strong stands on sexuality over the centuries.

One sexual problem can often affect several human needs. For example, infrequent sex in her marriage caused Diana anger, insomnia, low self-esteem (thinking that she may have lost her attractiveness for her husband Dan) and insecurity (worrying that Dan was going to leave her for another woman), a shaky identity as a woman, and a sense of powerlessness. In therapy she learned that Dan's problem was low libido caused by work stress, and this understanding helped to restore her self-esteem, security, and feminine identity. Also, we discussed how to manage his stress better and how she could help him with it. That gave her a sense of power and shifted her focus from thinking and feeling bad about the problem to working on the solution. These steps markedly reduced the effects of stress on his libido. Although his libido was back to normal, it was still not as strong as hers. Diana handled this difference well by encouraging Dan to show more affection which he did, and accepting what he could not change. This way of changing what can be changed and accepting what cannot be changed is what I call "applying the spirit of the serenity prayer." Let us now explore sex in relationship to various needs.

PROCREATIVE ASPECT OF SEX

Procreative aspects of sex have undergone dramatic change in the last century due to the availability of safe and effective birth control methods and the need for population control. The Catholic Church opposes artificial contraception but it accepts natural family planning which prevents pregnancy by limiting sexual intercourse to the woman's infertile days. At the 1993 Parliament of World Religions, the Dalai Lama said that despite the Buddhist view of every human birth as precious, there are too many precious people already in the world, and he advised nonviolent birth control measures. Islam accepts artificial birth control to space and limit the number of children but prohibits it for not having any children at all.

SEX AND RELATIONSHIPS

The combination of passion, intimacy, interdependence and commitment creates wonderfully exciting and enjoyable relationships. Passion is strong liking, desire for, or devotion to someone or something. Sexual passion is an essential element in romantic love and marital happiness. In marriages passion often fluctuates for various reasons, and some people mistake the ebb of passion as proof of having fallen out of love. While the commitment of true love transcends passion, passion deserves special care.

Variety spices up passion. The fifteenth-century Hindu sage Kalyana Malla, who promoted monogamy, noted that the main reason for marital separation and extramarital affairs is the lack of variety in the couple's sexual pleasure. He urged couples to use variety in love making, and claimed that by varying his sexual enjoyment with his wife, a man can live as if he had thirty-two wives. Passion of a partner enhances passion of the other. Excitement begets excitement.

Sexual fantasy is one way to increase passion. Exciting incidents from one's own life, as well as from books, TV, and movies can provide materials for one's fantasy. Except for fantasies that reinforce sexual problems, sexual fantasies do not seem to be harmful. One benefit of sexual fantasy is that it does not have to suit one's partner if one keeps it confidential. Sharing sexual fantasies may help to know and meet each other's sexual needs better, but one has to be careful to avoid hurting one's partner. I have had many cases where disclosure of sexual fantasy offended a partner and caused conflicts in their relationship. A wife left her husband who revealed fantasies about her sister. Many religious groups, including the Catholic Church, prohibit sexual fantasies and pornography.

Liking is an important aspect of passion. Liking can be enhanced by focusing attention on the likable and overlooking the not so likable aspects of one's partner. Partners can enhance passion by understanding each other's tastes and doing what each other likes and avoiding what the one of the partners hates. Most people, especially women, love hugs and kisses. *USA Today* (January 1, 2001) reported that in an Internet query of 100,000 kissers, three out of four women thought kissing was more intimate than having sex. Although this query result raises doubts, it reflects the importance of kissing.

SEX AND IDENTITY

Sex and identity involves three areas: gender identity (the sense of being male or female biologically), the social role of being masculine or feminine, and sexual orientation.

Transsexualism (a biological female experiencing herself to be really a male or vice versa) and transvestitism (cross dressing) are rare, and people with these problems need professional help. I often see two problems in sexuality caused by social role expectations: problems with initiating sex and problems related to visual sexual stimulation.

1. *Problems With Taking the Initiative.* Many of my patients complain that their partners hardly ever initiate sex, which makes them feel undesirable, uninteresting, or sexually unattractive. Frequency of sexual intimacy and intercourse are also often low in such relationships. Women more often complain of their male companions not initiating sex. While most men seem to enjoy seductiveness from their partners, some men with old-fashioned ideas consider seductive women to be cheap or trashy. Many people do not appreciate the fact that variety and spontaneity of initiating sex enrich intimacy and passion and are therefore quite desirable. Showing desire for one's partner by initiating sex can enhance the partner's sexual desire, sexual identity, and self-esteem. Self-esteem of both partners also can be enhanced by the partners taking turns in initiating sex. The initiator can feel good for stimulating the partner and the follower can feel good about being desired.

Some female patients were angry with their husbands for not initiating sex even after they discussed the issue with their husbands, pitched fits, and refused sex. Still the husbands stonewalled the issue and refused couples' therapy. So I encouraged the women to feel good that they are *capable* of taking the initiative and enjoy their sexual relationship as fully as possible instead of giving up sex because of one missing element. This approach worked much better.

2. *Problems with visual sexual stimulation.* While voyeurism--the problem of Peeping Toms--is a sexual deviation, sexual stimulation by visual sources between partners is common and normal. The book, *Sex In America: A Definitive Survey,* reports that watching partners undress is the sexual practice that is most appealing next to vaginal intercourse. This was more so in younger people, especially males, than older individuals. The partner who is undressing can enjoy the power and playfulness of it, but some people feel guilt or shame instead because of their unhealthy superegos.

Women's lingerie is an important item of visual sexual stimuli. If the wife likes to wear sexy lingerie and her husband considers it trashy or if the husband wishes his wife to wear such clothing and she is resistant, it is useful for both to discuss the matter, develop a better understanding, and find a mutually agreeable solution. Many women are very reluctant to act seductively, thinking their figure is not good, often based on unrealistic ideals of attractiveness. Instead of assuming, it is best to ask one's partner what stimulates or repels him or her.

An increasingly frequent problem is obesity and its impact on women's sexuality because of poor self image. Many women reject sex because of this and strain their marital bond, thereby adding one more problem in their lives. In such cases the women are better off being sexually active for all its benefits including burning off many calories. In the clinical situations I have encountered, obesity of their wives did not prevent husbands from enjoying sex with their spouses. Of course, if the wives lost their excess weight, it would enhance the couple's sexlife.

Pornography has become more popular with its easy availability. More men than women enjoy it, and many women feel cheated or demeaned when their male partners use such sexual stimulation. Addiction to pornography is harmful like other addictions.

The issues of homosexuality and bisexuality are too complex and controversial to be discussed in depth here. To deal with them using conscience, we have to view available information about these issues in the context of human sexuality and judge with reason and the spirit of the Golden Rule. I want to comment only on one misunderstanding I have noticed many times: many people view gentleness in boys as a weakness and a sign of homosexual tendency. This is a culturally distorted view. Some parents discouraged their sons from watching Mr. Rogers' program on public television fearing that the gentleness of Mr. Rogers would influence their boys to become gays. From a spiritual view, gentleness is good, especially when combined with healthy toughness. Gentleness in boys discourages development of macho personality and enhances heterosexual relationships if they reject distorted cultural notions.

Sex and Esteem

Inaccurate or outright wrong ideas linking sexuality and self-worth cause esteem problems for many. Some women mistakenly think they are abnormal if they do not reach orgasm through intercourse and they need direct stimulation of the clitoris. Some men are still hung up on how well-hung they are. With genital stimulation most men ejaculate within two to six minutes, but many consider it too short a length of time. Some others don't relax and enjoy sex because of their pride in keeping control and fear of losing that control. I tell such people that healthy control involves useful loosening up; otherwise, the result is physical and emotional constipation [they laugh and they get the point].

Tremendous burdens of unhealthy guilt and shame are many times associated with sex because of unrealistic social and religious ideals.

Strict superego often finds sexuality a convenient issue to punish people. On the other hand, as society becomes more permissive, a lack of healthy guilt for harmful sexual behaviors, and even unhealthy pride in sexual exploitation of others, is also noticeable. From a spiritual view, we can feel good in using our sexuality with love and wisdom, with discipline but not rigidity.

Sex and Pleasure

Orgasm, the peak of physical pleasure, lasts only three to fifteen seconds, but the buildup of sexual excitement provides less-intense pleasure for several minutes to several hours. Resolution of sexual excitement through orgasm is characterized by a sense of well-being and relaxation of muscles and mind. The resolution phase after orgasm provides a special chance to reinforce the bond to one's partner by affectionate touch and talk. The pleasurable relaxation after orgasm helps induce sleep.

Sexual pleasure can be enhanced by building up sexual desire and excitement using several approaches: romantic time, plenty of foreplay, involvement of various senses, sexual fantasy, and variety in intercourse. Romantic time together enjoying a dinner, movie, or visit to a garden stimulates a sense of closeness and sexual desire. Plenty of foreplay means a great deal of kissing, caressing, massaging, and stroking that the partners can enjoy. For many people kissing is very important, and it is so sad that many people won't do such a simple thing for their partners.

Including various senses adds to the pleasure of foreplay and intercourse. Besides touch and vision, we can involve smell, taste, and hearing. Watching the partner's arousal can be exciting. Perfumes or the smell of a clean body or fresh sweat can be stimulating. Taste of one's favorite flavors can be used in oral sex. Tongue kisses can be spiced up by first chewing spices, like cinnamon--known for its arousing aroma--cloves, etc. Music or playful or sexy talk can be sexually exciting.

Often what a partner does is what he or she would enjoy. When a wife complained about her husband pinching her, I suggested that she pinch him for his pleasure and show him how differently she wanted to be touched. It worked well.

Many people enjoy more intense pleasure if they had some sexual stimuli (from fantasy, suggestive call from spouse, reading or watching erotic material etc.) during the hours before having sex. Many others lose the intensity of sexual pleasure because of being bombarded by sexual stimuli often from media and other sources. One can tune in or tune out sexual stimuli depending on which choice is useful.

Temporary abstinence and prolonged intercourse by delaying orgasm can enhance sexual pleasure. Temporary abstinence is utilized in the Jewish tradition--the couple abstains during menstruation and one week after. This enhances the pleasure of the couple as they engage in sex again. In the Hindu and Buddhist practice of "tantric" sex, physical union is prolonged by delaying orgasm. With the man's penis inside his partner's vagina, they focus on rhythmic breathing, kissing, and enjoying general body contact with very little movement of the genital area. This practice prolongs pleasure and deepens intimacy. The position most suitable for this practice is the partners sitting comfortably on a bed or stool facing each other.

SEX AND POWER

Sex has the power to promote health by reducing stress, relieving pain, enhancing the immune system, and providing   emotional release and pleasure. Good sex can prolong life.

Sexual enjoyment reduces stress in four different ways. 1) It expends energy which burns calories and reduces obesity. A woman weighing 120 pounds can burn up to eight calories a minute by taking an active role in sexual intercourse. 2) Sex has a nice rhythm and provides a welcome break from physical exertions that don't allow us to move at a nice rhythmic pace. 3) The resolution phase after orgasm provides excellent relaxation and reinforces the calming side of our nervous system. Many people masturbate to release sexual as well as general tension of body and mind. 4) Enhanced sleep from sex relieves stress.

Sexual enjoyment also provides pain relief. Orgasm releases endorphins, the body's own natural painkillers. The relaxation and stress reduction benefits of sexual enjoyment also help relieve pain. Conditions such as aches and pains of arthritis, various symptoms of premenstrual syndrome, and headaches may be relieved by sexual pleasure. So instead of a headache being an excuse to say "no," it can be an additional reason to go ahead and enjoy sex. But then the issue is whether one is in the mood to enjoy sex. While mood can motivate our behavior, one can use ones imagination and willpower deliberately to bring about a desirable mood. If we try and fail at creating the desirable mood, we can still feel good about our attempt.

Increased levels of oxytocin associated with orgasm reduces stress and decreases risk of breast cancer. The hormone DHEA, also released during orgasm, reduces the risk of heart disease. Regular sexual activity helps to relieve menstrual cramps, regulate menstrual cycles, enhance immune systems, and prevent chronic non-bacterial prostatitis.

A ten year follow up study published in the *British Medical Journal* in December 1997 found that men who had at least two orgasms a week had less than half the risk of dying from various causes compared to men who had orgasm less frequently. Also, it has been known that men who ejaculate regularly have less chance of prostate cancer.

A good sex life helps tremendously in providing corrective emotional experience to heal old sexual traumas and enhance body image, self-esteem, and sense of power.

When sex is used harmfully or unfairly as a tool for power and control over others, it is emotionally and spiritually unhealthy. Some people enjoy the power and control of denying affection and sex to their spouses and there are others who like the power of manipulative or violent sexuality. These choices are very unhealthy for both heart and soul. Seduction by false promises or pretenses is a common manipulation. Forced or coerced sex is the worst use of sex for power and pleasure. Communities that accept aggression and violence as part of masculinity have far higher rates of rape. The more violent a community or an individual is, the more chances for combining sex and violence. In the *Sex in America Survey*, about 3% of men found the idea of forced sex appealing. Also 3% of men admitted that they had forced someone to have sex.

SEX AND INTEGRATING THE PAST

In integrating the past in sexuality, my clinical experience has been in dealing with sexual abuse and affairs that have already ended or almost ended.

Childhood sexual abuse or sexual abuse by someone including a boyfriend or a spouse needs healing. Talking about the abuse and the negative feelings associated with these memories is extremely important. Putting the past in perspective with the help of therapy is very useful. The principles I discussed in integrating the past can be applied to sexual traumas. Forgiveness or reconciliation are important, but becoming obsessed with the traumatic issues and getting stuck with anger or depression is not useful. It is important to keep the hope alive that if one has survived the real experience, one can surmount the memory too. Also it is crucial to deal with any ongoing unhealthy tendency (such as choosing abusive partners or being hyper-sexed or averse to sex) instead of focusing too much on the past. Individual and group therapy can be very useful, but getting stuck in therapy does not help either.

Sexual affairs are often ways in which people try to meet many needs, not just sexual pleasure or affection. Patients who had an isolated sexual liaison, particularly under special circumstances, and have guilt/shame about it seem to learn from the experience and become stronger and more committed in their marital relationship. They progressed as they used their conscience, examined their experience carefully, and learned about their needs and how to meet them in better ways. But people who habitually have affairs or have no regrets about an affair seem not to learn and grow from the experience. Also people who moralistically wallow in guilt without taking a broader view of life seem to miss the chance to transform.

Expert opinions vary regarding whether to confess to the spouse who was cheated. One has to consider seriously the consequences of confessing to an unsuspecting spouse or to a spouse who would use the information destructively. Confession is good for the soul but as the AA teaches, confess to self, to God, and to a fellow human being. In confessing to a person, one has to choose someone who will keep confidentiality because many people like to gossip, and, some individuals enjoy causing problems for others. Then reflect on what is the constructive, fair, and loving thing to do; seek advice from a dependable person if needed, and decide. In my practice, many individuals did not confess to spouses but worked out their problems with therapy, as they believed confessing would be destructive. Many people who confessed to unsuspecting or vengeful spouses regretted the suffering that resulted from their confession.

One man had a liaison for a few weeks while he was under much stress and was lonely because he was working outside the country and his wife was not with him for couple of years. He confessed to his wife long after the affair, and she reacted badly. The marriage survived, but the couple suffered for years, with no apparent benefit from the confession.

If the cheated spouse knows or is likely to find out about the affair, it seems wise to confess, express regret, and discuss the reasons for the affair as well as the positive changes the cheater has made and steps the couple can take to prevent an affair in future. The unfaithful spouse can take the steps of realistic guilt explained in Chapter Five. The victim can forgive or reconcile as described in Chapter Nine. The saying, "once a cheater, always a cheater" is not true in my clinical experience. While affairs go against conscience, people who had an isolated affair in special circumstances (not habitual affairs) and had realistic guilt/shame seem to be individuals who live by their consciences in general.

MASTURBATION

While Hippocrates, the father of modern medicine, believed sexual intercourse and masturbation weaken the body, another great physician, Galen (second century A.D.) held the opposite view which is favored by modern medicine. Eleventh century Muslim philosopher Avicenna advised masturbation when sexual intercourse was impossible.

In 1710 an English physician, Dr. Bekkers incorrectly called masturbation Onanism, after Onan (Genesis 38:7-10) who was punished by God for spilling his semen when he had sex with the widow of his late brother. Onan did so to prevent her from bearing a child who could inherit his brother's property; his sin was that he broke the custom of inheritance, not masturbation. For several centuries, medical science attributed many physical and psychological disorders to masturbation. Several amusing attempts to cure masturbation included J.H. Kellogg's corn flakes, Sylvester Graham's dietary plan, and someone's invention of a genital cage that sounded an alarm if a boy had an erection.

Karl Menninger had examined many state mental hospital records and found that masturbation was considered the cause of many of those cases. Menninger noted that people's attitude changed dramatically in the twentieth century: "... this ancient taboo, for the violation of which millions had been punished, threatened, condemned...vanished almost overnight. Masturbation... suddenly seemed not so sinful, perhaps not sinful at all; not so dangerous—-in fact not dangerous at all; less a vice than a pleasurable experience, and a normal and healthy one!"[44]

Among the participants of the *Sex in America* survey about 25% of men and 10% of women masturbate at least once a week, and 60% of men and 40% of women masturbated in the previous year. Very significantly, the rate of masturbation was higher among couples living together--85% for men and 45% for women--indicating that the more active one's sex life, the more likely it would include masturbation.

In dealing with several thousand patients over the years, I recall only three cases (besides a few exhibitionists and sex addicts) where the person's masturbation was noticeably harmful except for religious or cultural conflicts. In each of the three cases the man's masturbation often deprived his wife of intercourse, even on the wedding night in one case. But in numerous cases people experienced masturbation as useful although many had inner conflicts about it because their religion (Catholic Church and many others) condemned it.

Sexuality, Religion/spirituality, and Conscience

The relationship between sexuality and spirituality has been confused for centuries because of religious, cultural, and medical misunderstandings. Using one's sexuality in ways that are harmful or unfair violates conscience and is clearly wrong, but many religious groups have sexual standards that are stricter or looser than this. It is useful to know what exactly one's religion teaches about sex, the reasoning behind it, and historically how the teaching came about. Such information provides crucial input into our consciences.

From a spiritual view, one must not go against one's conscience, but one can go beyond the requirements of conscience and live by a stricter religious or personal ideal if it is beneficial. An example is a couple who practice mutually agreed temporary celibacy as a spiritual exercise. During the period of celibacy, they evaluate the real results and are ready to discontinue the practice if the results are unhealthy or either of them wants sex.

The Catholic Church accepts sex for pleasure within marriage. The church objects to artificial contraception on the basis that according to the natural law (the divinely ordained goal of something) sex is for procreation and any sexual act that artificially prevents the chance of conception is sinful. Oral sex and mutual masturbation are accepted as part of foreplay but considered sins if carried on to ejaculation outside the vagina. I know many Catholics who follow their own consciences and use contraceptives and some Catholics who happily practice natural family planning.

Among Protestant Christian writers, Lewis Smedes does not reject masturbation unless it causes problems such as avoidance of marital sex, and James Dobson notes that the Bible does not address this issue except in the Onan story which really is not about masturbation. Protestant Christian churches differ about sexual values, but in general they oppose adultery, incest, and prostitution; homosexuality has become a controversial issue in many denominations.

There is a view that pleasure, not procreation, is the more pervasive natural driving force in human sexuality. Clearly human sexuality is far more extensive than needed for, or tied to, procreation. For women sexual desire and pleasure persist when they are infertile. Thus, human sexuality is, by nature, different from that of animals whose sexual urge and pleasure are, in general, closely tied to procreation. Moreover, the clitoris, the most pleasure inducing female organ, is the only human organ with the sole function of pleasure. Pleasure as the dominant natural aspect of human sexuality is not just a modern or a secular idea either--for several millennia Hinduism has taught satisfaction of sexual pleasure as one of the four goals (the other goals are material well-being, ethical living, and ultimate liberation) of life. Sexual pleasure greatly enhances human pair bonding. Judaism and Islam celebrate sexual pleasure within legitimate relationships.

The Tibetan Buddhist psychiatry--claimed to be the world's oldest psychiatry--in many cases advises the patient to have sex. For instance, in many cases when a person is constantly thinking and talking about sex, the problem is due to desire. "Sexual relations may help a person by satisfying desire and are therefore prescribed along with medicines."[45] And in traditional Chinese medicine, good sex is considered a tonic for health and happiness.

People have realistic reason for guilt and shame if they use sexuality in harmful or unfair ways including unreasonably withholding sex. Many people lack such healthy guilt and shame. Not uncommonly, people feel unhealthy guilt and shame about sexual actions and thoughts because of religious or cultural ideas that they have not examined using well-informed consciences. Several patients who gained broad knowledge about sexuality and used their consciences overcame their unhealthy guilt and shame. Still others developed a healthy sense of guilt and shame about abusing or not properly using their sexuality.

A couple had sexual conflicts because the wife could reach orgasm only with direct stimulation of her clitoris from oral sex or using a vibrator. The husband thought such activities were unnatural and wrong, and his wife's problem had hurt his male ego. He followed my recommendation to read about sex and became aware that his wife's orgasmic difficulty did not reflect poorly on his manliness, and that her use of direct clitoral stimulation was very useful and fair, and therefore in harmony with conscience.

A female patient expressed her disgust with the doggie position of intercourse which her husband wanted sometimes: "It is such a humiliating thing--on all fours, looking down like a dumb animal about to eat filth." She had picked up the idea from her church that only the missionary position was sinless, and her imagination added aversive images to the doggie position. Asked whether she liked seeing puppies playing and whether she liked Chinese food for a change, she answered affirmatively. After discussing about the benefits of play and variety in sex, and how the old Christian position on sexual positions had formed, she used her conscience and enjoyed a far better, more varied sex life.

Another patient was averse to acting seductively with her husband because she associated such behavior with prostitution. But her attitude changed as she learned about the benefits of playfulness and of visual stimulation, and listened to her conscience instead of her superego.

A man thought he was living by his conscience in his marriage because he was faithful. He had sexual urge only couple of times a month and ignored his wife's pleas for sex more often which he could do if he wanted. He had stronger need for more tasty food than his wife did, and she had accommodated his extra need. I asked him to imagine how he would feel if his wife would not put the extra effort to meet his dietary needs, and to apply the spirit of the Golden Rule in dealing with her sexual need. As he did this, he realized that living by his conscience would involve deeper understanding and more efforts to meet his wife's needs. As he tried, they had a happier relationship.

Sexuality can enhance our capacity for empathy if we broaden our understanding of our own and others' sexuality—-recognizing feelings, thoughts, actions, and reactions, and the connection of sexuality to other needs. The stronger our empathy, the better we understand the difference in other's needs. Many individuals empathize with another's pain, especially obvious pain, but not another's pleasure, if it is different from their own. As we expand our empathy, we enhance our compassion and love. By being aware of what other human need (for example, esteem, power or identity) is closely tied to one's own and one's partner's sexuality one can pay special attention to meet that need. A woman was able to enjoy orgasm after two decades of marriage when I helped her to recognize her intense need for control and security connected with her sexuality, and the couple worked together to meet those needs. Benevolence in bed can be a part of charity beginning at home.

Those who live by their consciences would take measures to prevent sexually transmitted disease, unwanted pregnancy, and other bad consequences for themselves or others and get the benefits of healthy sex. Many naively trusting people catch sexually transmitted diseases from very selfish partners who do not use protection and pretend they are safe. Some unscrupulous women pretend that they are on birth control pills and deliberately get pregnant.

Many couples have no, or hardly any, "intramarital" sex, because one partner stubbornly rejects sex but is often proud of being faithful. This is what I call "half faithfulness." While not committing adultery, the spouses who reject sex are depriving themselves and are quite unfair to their partners who want sex. Such cold spouses who are guided by their twisted superegos often become hotly contemptuous if the frustrated partner strays. Although the issues involved are quite different, we won't consider a man as our "faithful" employ for not working for somebody else, if he doesn't do our work either. People with sexual dysfunctions would seek help, especially if their spouses desire sex, if they use their consciences.

Those who choose celibate lives for religious reasons can find overall psychological and spiritual fulfillment by channeling their energies more into healthy satisfaction of other needs, especially by pursuing deep spiritual meaning. I have closely known many such people. However, if the ideal of celibacy is unrealistic for a person, it is crucial for the individual to be realistic and not act like Dr. Jekyll.

Sex can involve a transcendent experience. During sex one can transcend the usual sense of self and have a feeling of merging with one's partner. During orgasm one may experience a sense of transcending time and space and merging with the universe. Many people experience a spiritual presence some times while making love. And many view sexual love as a symbol of Divine Love.

Our sexuality offers us wonderful chances to exercise discipline, empathy, compassion, pleasure, love, and wisdom by using this great gift with conscience in fulfilling ways.

13. Live Meaningfully

"I have seen many people die because life for them was not worth living. From this I conclude that the question of life's meaning is the most urgent question of all."[46]

Albert Camus

Having a sense of meaning, purpose, or significance makes life worth living. Without a sense of meaning--an overall view of what life is all about--we get distressed and tend to give up, sometimes permanently. Our sense of meaning or our beliefs about life's purpose and value evolves from what we learn from family and community and other sources of knowledge and from our interpretation of our experiences. We may lose our old sense of meaning in times of crisis but gain new meaning as we deal with the crisis. Our interpretation of experiences is often highly influenced by others close to us and by leaders whose ideas we accept. Our sense of meaning can be either secular or spiritual, and in either case it can be superficial or deep. Conscience helps to choose a good system of meaning as well as to live by it.

The Need for Meaning

The idea that life is a bitch and then you die is dramatized in Shakespeare's *Macbeth* (Act 5, scene 5):

"Life's but a walking shadow; a poor player,
That struts and frets his hour upon the stage,
And then is heard no more: it is a tale
Told by an idiot, full of sound and fury,

Signifying nothing."

This sense of the meaninglessness of life is particularly ironic since it is spoken by the ambitious Macbeth who had assassinated King Duncan to gain power and glory. The materialistic dreams of Macbeth and his cunning wife had turned into depressing nightmares. Macbeth could have had a rich and meaningful life had he searched for more power and meaning guided by his conscience.

French philosopher Jean Paul Sartre expressed similar meaninglessness about life: "All existing things are born for no reason, continue through weakness and die by accident.... It is meaningless that we are born; it is meaningless that we die."[47] Sartre did not give up on life, however, but continued to seek meaning by commitment to literature, philosophy, and social activism, thereby becoming a prominent intellectual of his time and a Nobel Prize winner for Literature.

Carl Jung and Viktor Frankl have stated that a significant number of their patients suffered from meaninglessness. I have found that many of my patients have an increased need for meaning when they face crises and their old sense of meaning is shattered. Most people can pick up the pieces of their shattered meaning, discard the useless parts, add new insights, and form a broader, deeper sense of meaning.

I saw this happen in Gary, a young man who was hospitalized following a suicide attempt precipitated by his wife's filing for divorce. Gary had a habit of lying and telling half-truths or "shading the truth," as he put it. He used to keep his wife mostly in the dark about his finances and had lost money in some risky ventures but continued to take unnecessary risks. Gary's wife had threatened divorce before, but Gary kept on denying or minimizing his problems until his wife actually filed for divorce. His suicide attempt was partly a cry for help and partly a last-ditch effort to stop his wife from leaving him. His wife stood her ground, and once Gary realized he had lost her, he focused on developing new meaning for his life.

Previously Gary had found meaning in meeting his own needs, especially self-esteem, power, and pleasure by manipulating others, and he had no guilt or shame about his lies, manipulations, irresponsibility, and selfishness. Having grown up in an affluent family with strong materialistic and superficial religious values, he attended church for social rather than spiritual reasons. His fashionable car was part of his identity.

In the process of divorce and on shaky grounds financially, Gary realized how much he had hurt his wife, who had given him numerous chances to change. He first tried to convince her that he would change so she would stop the divorce proceedings. When this strategy failed, Gary's crisis intensified; he worked more seriously to understand the flaws in his meaning and values and to change for the better. He read and reflected on spiritual meaning and understood the deeper aspects of his religion. Most importantly, he began to listen to and follow the guidance of his conscience, which led him to a new sense of meaning, self-esteem, and fulfillment.

Numerous religious groups and a multiplicity of secular groups promote their brand of meaning indicating the tremendous human need for meaning and the lack of any uniform meaning system. Rick Warren's book, *The Purpose Driven Life* which promotes the belief that everyone is born by and for God's purpose, has sold over twenty million copies, showing the popularity of such a meaning.

THE SEARCH FOR MEANING

As in Gary's case, suffering is often closely connected with development of better meaning. When we lose our old belief system, say in a crisis, we often experience depression. Interestingly, the word for "depression" used by a Patagonian Indian tribe means the crab that has lost its shell and has not yet formed a new shell. Our belief system functions as a framework, and when we lose the old framework, we often become emotionally disoriented and depressed. This type of depression, but not all depressions, can be useful since it can motivate us to find new meaning.

Instead of depression, some people experience anxiety from the fear of the unknown as they give up their familiar meanings. In a crisis involving our sense of meaning, we are torn between the wish to return to the comfort of the familiar, although flawed, meaning and the urge to go forward with a new and better, but unfamiliar, meaning. Fear of the unknown often discourages people from pursing something different. Moral courage and intellectual curiosity can help to explore and cautiously expand one's meaning. Unfortunately, many people choose the comfort of the old rather than the benefits of the new.

If a person's existing meaning system involves strong fear about any modification, then the individual finds it very difficult to explore other meanings. This is usually the case with people who are conditioned by rigid, narrow religious or cultural beliefs. Often such people are scared to death of going to hell if they even explore another worldview. Those who have deeply examined their religious or other belief system in the light of conscience, however, may have no need to reevaluate their meaning even when they face a serious crisis. In fact, a strong and deep meaning helps people to handle crisis much better.

Unhealthy pride in our current belief system is another reason we resist changing it. We often pick up a frame of meaning--and a sense of comfort and pride about it--from our family and society as we grow up, and many people do not give serious consideration to meaning unless a crisis or an intense experience shakes up the old meaning and stimulates a search for deeper meaning.

The Buddha experienced this kind of crisis and the need to search for the deeper meaning of life. Whether one agrees or disagrees with the Buddha's teachings, his spiritual journey itself is instructive. Siddhartha Gautama, later called The Buddha, was a prince who lived in India in the sixth century B. C. Based on a prediction that if this prince were exposed to suffering, he would become a great teacher rather than a great king, his father protected him from exposure to suffering. Thus Siddhartha lived a superficial life of ease and pleasure until he was twenty-nine when he went outside the palace walls and saw four sights that shattered his previous meaning of life: an old person, a sick man, a dead body being carried for cremation--all of which depicted suffering--and a wandering sage, who reflected inner joy and peace.

Siddhartha immediately knew that his mission in life was to solve the riddle of suffering, and he left his palace and began a period of wandering learning meditation and self-discipline. He later joined a band of ascetics but left them after six years because asceticism did not help him to achieve his goal. He then sat under a huge bodhi tree and meditated for forty-nine days. He was tempted by fear, desire, pleasure, and passion, but did not succumb to them. On the forty-ninth day Siddhartha understood the cause and cure of suffering. He described his new condition as being awake, thus becoming known as the Buddha or the "Enlightened One."

The Buddha's story demonstrates several important points about the search for meaning. Having experienced and rejected both the pleasures of palace life and the pains of asceticism, the Buddha preached and practiced the Middle Way, reminiscent of the Golden Mean of Aristotle and Confucius. Satisfaction with a superficial, materialistic existence is easily damaged by facing the tragic dimensions and broader realities of life. New meaning can arise from the chaos caused by the destruction of the old. Many people tend to go from one extreme to another in the search for meaning, but moderation is the way to fulfillment. Overcoming, not succumbing to, the temptations of fear, pleasure, and desire are essential to spiritual growth. Our compassionate response to suffering enhances and ennobles our meaning. We do not need to create artificial suffering by asceticism or masochism; there already is plenty of suffering in the world. If one has the capacity and desire to take on more than one's natural suffering, one can share somebody else's rather than create more suffering.

Here I recall the story of Lee Atwater, the Republican Party Chairman who had helped former President George H. W. Bush to win the election. Shortly before his death from brain tumor in 1991, Atwater wrote an article in *Life* magazine about his spiritual transformation. He was materialistic and had acquired more power, prestige, and wealth than most people but felt empty. Faced with death he searched for and found the common ground of religions--the Golden Rule. He made a commitment to the Golden Rule and promoted the ideals of human heart and brotherhood which he observed were missing in him before and missing in our society. He urged leaders to address the spiritual vacuum in America caught up in ruthless ambition.

SOURCES OF MEANING

People gain a sense of meaning from various sources, including parents, teachers, community leaders, peers, mass media, spiritual and philosophical ideas, certain scientific theories, myths and traditions of various cultures, and religious teachings.

Myths have been an important source of meaning in various cultures for thousands of years. Myths are not falsehoods, unless we take them literally, but if we take their underlying meanings, we gain insight into deeper truths of life. Myths and parables are meant for our imagination to understand deeper meanings. Joseph Campbell's ideas popularized by Bill Moyers on public television and Jungian psychology have promoted interest in mythology.

In traditional cultures, many festivals have mythical connotations. These celebrations meet the need for pleasure and for social relationship, reinforce the group identity, and give meaning to life. Joseph Campbell rejects the notion that seasonal festivals of the native peoples are efforts to control natural forces. He observes: "...the dominant motive in all truly religious (as opposed to black magical) ceremonies is that of submission to the inevitables of destiny--and in the seasonal festivals, this motive is particularly apparent."[48]

A sense of destiny is an integral part of the meaning system of many people, especially religious groups. Although religions differ in ideas about the meaning of life, they basically agree that a spiritual realm exists and that we must live in harmony with it. Aldous Huxley proposed that a perennial philosophy underlies the meaning systems of the great world religions. According to the perennial philosophy, there is a divine Reality underlying the world of things and beings, the human soul is something similar to or identical with the divine Reality (this is our spiritual nature), and our ultimate goal and greatest good is the realization of our spiritual nature.[49]

For psychological health, any philosophy of life that gives meaning to the individual is fine; spiritual health, however, involves spiritual meaning. Many healthy variations on the basic theme of spiritual meaning exist, and people can authentically pursue their own paths--or follow their own bliss to borrow a phrase from Joseph Campbell. Sometimes it may be a heartache or even a breakthrough from a breakdown that leads to a special meaning to one's life.

Many observers believe that a sense of meaninglessness has worsened in recent decades because of industrialization and people's distancing from nature and natural processes. In agrarian societies people are more in contact with the process of birth, stages of growth, death and decay of plants and animals, and are more aware of the seasonal changes. Living close to nature provides an underlying sense of meaning, although it may be fuzzy intellectually.

Viktor Frankl, who spent three years in a Nazi concentration camp, and has written extensively on meaning, observes in *Man's Search for Meaning* that we discover meaning by achievements and accomplishments; by experiencing something, like nature or work, and relating to someone in loving relationship; and by having a positive attitude towards suffering. Frankl's attitude about his suffering was that only by surviving the concentration camp could he complete his work. This attitude helped him tremendously in dealing with his sufferings at the camp and its memories later. Many of his fellow prisoners found meaning in surviving for the sake of others like family members, or to complete a work. He found that suffering can have a meaning if it changes a person for the better. According to Frankl, everyone has a specific mission in life that must be carried out to fulfill one's life.

Frankl rejects Abraham Maslow's idea that higher needs such as the need to know, emerge only when basic needs like the need for food are satisfied: "Maslow's distinction between higher and lower needs does not take into account that when lower needs are *not* satisfied, a higher need, such as the will to meaning, may become most urgent.

...who would deny that in such circumstances [as in death camps and deathbeds] the thirst for meaning, even ultimate meaning, breaks through irresistibly?"[50] Maslow's idea, however, has merit too; for example, even usually calm and loving people may become irritable and hostile if they miss sleep and food. As the old saying goes, a hungry man is an angry man.

Meanings can be either a secular one which excludes belief in a spiritual realm or a religious/spiritual one which includes belief in a spiritual realm. Both the secular and the spiritual or religious meanings can be on a superficial or a deep level.

SUPERFICIAL SECULAR MEANING

People who have a superficial secular meaning in life give excessive importance to appearances, fashions, and fads. Their knowledge, relationships, interests, commitments, and identity are shallow. They block out spiritual needs; they meet their physical and psychological needs by superficial, often selfish, means. They are prone to petty jealousies and silly comparisons. Keeping up with the Jones' and following the cultural in-things may be the ultimate concerns for them. They may be passionate about certain hobbies or politics without broader outlook and deeper understanding of life.

Many individuals with superficial secular meaning do function fairly as members of society but they sadly miss the human potential for living in depth. Their openness to goodness, love, and wisdom are very limited. They may have strong attachment to many of their own needs and selfish or superficial ways of meeting those needs. They also contribute much to the mediocrity in society. Suffering from unfulfilled potentials, they can easily become addicts or followers of extremist ideologies or groups. Their empathy and compassion are superficial and limited to their families, friends and groups with whom they closely identify. They are prone to prejudge, misunderstand people who are different and hate people who are easily perceived as enemies.

They may exploit others and neglect their responsibilities (for example, fathers who do not pay child support but spend lavishly on party girls). Many people with personality disorders or character defects show this meaning schema. Materialism and superficial secular meaning go hand in hand. Superficial spiritual (often religious) meaning and materialism also reinforce each other. Such are the superstitious and magical religious approaches that neglect goodness and promote power and prestige.

The sensualistic approach of "do whatever makes you feel good right now" is often a part of various addictions, crime, and violence. Many people can easily get caught up in the superficial life style because of its glitz and glamour, hedonism, cheap sense of power, superficial identity, and false pride.

If we use our curiosity, social awareness, historical perspective, creative imagination, and our consciences to any great extent, we cannot remain superficial. Using various defenses and being immersed just in materialistic pursuits or trivialities of life, however, one can maintain a superficial secular meaning.

People with superficial meaning are at high risk to become severely depressed if they loose the source of their meager meaning. One man who grew up in poverty had made material success by hard work his meaning in life. After midlife, he could not work following an accident and he became deeply depressed. He could manage fairly financially and he did not suffer physical pain. His depression was mostly from losing his sense of meaning. Although he was very resistant at first to examine his belief that the purpose of a man is to work and make money for a good living, he gradually opened his mind and developed a deep spiritual meaning and overcame his deep depression.

DEEPER SECULAR MEANING

Deep involvement in life processes, creative work, commitment to a good cause, altruism and self-actualization, and living by secular principles of human responsibilities and rights are examples of deeper secular meaning. Those who are deeply involved in nature's process of growth, fruition, death and decay, and the change of seasons, and so on, like farmers, can easily have a deep meaning in life and an intrinsic sense of worth to their work. They can also do their work superficially or mindlessly, without deeper engagement and enjoyment, paying no attention to the mysteries they closely encounter, and envying those who live by cleverly browbeating others. Raising children and working in the helping or healing professions provide opportunities to tune in to the life processes and issues of suffering and growth. Here too one can work and live superficially.

So, it is not just one's daily activities or line of work as such but the attitude with which one takes one's experiences that makes a big difference in one's meaning. A reflective attitude is crucial for deeper meaning, and contacts with people who are reflective stimulate our own capacity for the same. With a reflective attitude, as we apply our knowledge in practical situations our meaning deepen. A story about a great Islamic teacher Bahaudin Naqshband illustrates this point. A student tried different teachers and gathered much knowledge before coming to him. After some discussion Naqshband gave him a big meal. The student ate excessively and in a short time he suffered the pains of indigestion. Naqshband told him that instead of stuffing too much knowledge as he did with the food, he should digest and absorb the teachings by applying it in his life. As the student followed this advice, he gained true spiritual wisdom which involves deep spiritual meaning. Previously the student had misinterpreted his spiritual indigestion as hunger for more knowledge.

Books, radio, and television programs that stimulate a broader understanding of life also help in developing deeper meaning. As we establish a habit of reflection or contemplation, we can appreciate Aristotle's idea that contemplation is the highest of activities. Creative work such as arts and crafts, writing, and scientific research can involve people deeply in life.

Commitment to a good cause is a great method to make life meaningful. The greater the cause, the deeper the meaning. The cause may be social, political, religious, scientific, or artistic but it goes beyond self-interest and enhances goodness, truth or beauty.

Service to others, or altruism, is both a secular and spiritual method of finding deeper meaning. All the world religions instruct their followers to transcend their selfishness and help the needy. It has been consistently found that altruistic individuals are happier than the self-centered ones. A physician friend told me of a lady who adopted a severely mentally retarded child who is also disfigured from physical abuse and has multiple chronic illnesses. When other people ask this woman why she took on such an enormously difficult task, she tells them that taking care of this child makes her life fulfilling.

SELF-ACTUALIZATION

Self-actualization can be on a secular or spiritual level. Abraham Maslow popularized the concept of self-actualization, i.e., one actually reaching and living according to one's true potential, an idea that goes back to Aristotle. An artist who is not doing artistic work or a poet who is not producing poetry is missing his or her true potential; they are alienated from their own true selves.

Such alienation stifles life and causes unhappiness.

Maslow's study of self-actualizing people including Lincoln, Jefferson, Einstein, Spinoza, Martin Buber, and William James[51] showed characteristics such as
- more efficient perception of reality
- acceptance of self, others, and nature
- spontaneity and simplicity
- some mission in life
- positive liking of solitude
- deeper and more profound interpersonal relationships
- wonderful capacity to appreciate the basic goods of life
- genuine desire to help humanity
- humility
- gentle sense of humor
- ethical strength

Maslow included peak experiences also as a feature of self-actualizing people. Every aspect of peak-experience, according to Maslow, can be listed as religious happenings. Of the twenty-five religious aspects of peak-experiences Maslow listed, the last one clearly refers to the sense of the sacred: "What has been called the 'unitive consciousness' is often given in peak-experiences, i.e., a sense of the sacred glimpsed in and through the particular instance of the momentary, the secular, the worldly."[52]

Altruism and self-actualization are part of the deep secular and deep spiritual meaning systems. Interestingly, those who have either of these deep meaning systems have a great deal in common--such as psychological mindedness, openness to goodness, tragic sense with realistic hope, integrated rather than compartmentalized views, and eagerness to use wisdom. Psychological mindedness goes beyond the view that one can increase a behavior by rewards and decrease it by punishments. Even without knowing psychological theories, people with deeper meaning have openness to understand by observing, listening, reflecting and finding patterns why somebody is behaving in a certain way. They are open to learning from others. They are open to goodness and rejects evil even when it is done by their own group. Tragic sense involves awareness of human suffering caused by accidents, sickness, natural disasters, and misfortune. Tragic sense is coupled with realistic hope and sense of human dignity. Integrated view and wisdom involves viewing an issue from various angles and recognizing the practical choices and limitations. The biggest difference among the four types of meaning is between those who have the superficial secular meaning and the ones who have deep spiritual meaning.

SUPERFICIAL SPIRITUAL/RELIGIOUS MEANING

A common phenomenon is those people who have a very narrow understanding of their religion and follow it superficially. They have a closed mind and often have magical and superstitious beliefs and practices mixed with spirituality. They are deficient in love and wisdom, and show excessive fear, need for control, and tendency to manipulate. Many such people are connected with religious institutions and participate in religious activities without learning the deeper meanings of religious teachings and practices. They go through the motions for comfort, social approval or other emotional reasons.

These individuals use various defenses described in Chapter Three. They also tend to be not psychologically minded. They either do not have or do not use psychological insights to understand themselves, others, and life better.

Depending on their superego's judgment they may feel no guilt about something really unfair they did to a person of a different faith. Or they may feel excessive guilt about a fleeting sexual thought that they take as very sinful. When they do something really harmful to somebody, they may not use the process of healthy guilt as noted in Chapter Five; they may just vanish the guilt with a confession to God or a clergy.

Also they do not use their intellectual abilities to understand and evaluate their beliefs and other beliefs in depth. Such people often believe in dogmas, ideas or ideals that clearly contradict scientific proofs and ethical principles. They often have very limited and biased information about their own faith. Their knowledge about other religions is either poor or distorted to fit their narrow outlook, and often an unreasonable sense of superiority. Some religious fanatics have a great deal of distorted information that supports their attitude but not a balanced understanding. Such superficial meaning system tends to go with false pride and it can easily cause suspiciousness, contempt, meanness, and hate toward people with other worldviews.

Religious reformers have fought against various aspects of superficial religiosity which cater to the hunger for meaning by providing easy answers and quick fixes. There are religious leaders who manipulate this thirst and enrich their own power and prestige. Even the superficial faiths give a sense of direction and purpose in life, and so it is better than the despair of meaninglessness. People with either superficial or deep religious meaning benefit from hopes of good lives hereafter. Such hopes help people to accept their sufferings here better. At the same time, some of them may feel tormented by fear of hell.

DEEPER SPIRITUAL/RELIGIOUS MEANING

Religions teach the existence of a spiritual realm that transcends the material universe. They often teach the existence of a Higher Power. This Higher Power is considered in personal terms in Judaism, Christianity, and Islam (Yahweh, the Heavenly Father, and Allah, respectively) and not in personal terms in Hinduism and Taoism (Brahman and Tao respectively). Buddhism believes in a spiritual realm, karma, reincarnation, and nirvana but not in God.

In their depths the great world religions emphasize overcoming one's superficiality and selfishness, and living in harmony with one's spiritual or higher self, with others, and with the Ultimate Reality. Ethical living, self-discipline, promotion of goodness, and cultivation of wisdom are the practical approaches to reach these goals. Living by a deep spiritual meaning produces the fruits of peace, joy, harmony, hope, openness of mind, respect for truth, and loving/compassionate relationships.

Whatever faith one follows, for the purpose of deeper meaning it is crucial to know the important teachings and the history of one's faith. Also it is useful to have some true knowledge--not false notions in favor or against--about the other major worldviews. Many people in our times enrich their spiritual lives by adapting ideas and practices from different sources. In my view, living by deeper meaning and conscience is important for spiritual strength.

Challenges by different worldviews can stimulate deeper meaning. The life of historian William Shirer--who wrote about Hitler, the embodiment of hate, Gandhi, the apostle of love, and Tolstoy's love-hate marital bond--provides an example of spiritual growth of a person who was deeply exposed to different cultures and worldviews. In *Gandhi A Memoir*, Shirer states that he considered Gandhi his greatest teacher, and the most important lesson he learned from Gandhi was to seek Truth and avoid hypocrisy. He also learned that regular practice of contemplation and living a life of self-discipline--keeping greed, lust, selfishness, and worldly ambition in control--were important for maintaining spiritual strength. Shirer found Gandhi's approach to learning from the deeper meanings of various faiths very rewarding. Shirer's narrow Presbyterian upbringing had dulled his capacity to be deeply spiritual, but Gandhi's influence helped him gain a deeper appreciation for Christianity and opened his eyes to the wisdom of Hinduism, Buddhism, and Islam.

Studies of people who have had near-death experience (NDE) show that they become deeply spiritual as a result of the experience. A study of fifty-three subjects who had NDE with a control group who had similar life-threatening incidents without NDE showed that while both groups had undergone changes, those who had NDE had considerably greater changes. The changes following NDE include a reduction in death anxiety, a stronger belief in afterlife, greater concern for others, greater transcendental feelings, reduction in materialism, increased self-worth, more appreciation of nature, and greater awareness of paranormal phenomenon.[53]

While any kind of meaning can reduce one's sense of meaninglessness and the anxiety from it, the deeper meaning systems help us to live more happily and harmoniously, both individually and collectively. Just as a tree with deep roots is not easily uprooted by the winds, a deep meaning system can withstand the ravages of time and crises. In my experience, people with deep spiritual meaning seem to be more fulfilled than those with deep secular meaning but I must confess that I know far more people of the former than the latter type. In the words of William James, "...in a merely human world without God [or a spiritual realm, I would add], the appeal to our moral energy falls short of its maximal stimulating power."[54]

We are strongly influenced by the prevailing attitudes and ideas of our times. That is natural and normal so long as we also give enough importance to the time-tested and lasting secular and spiritual meanings.

HOW TO HAVE A GOOD MEANING SYSTEM

It is important to examine what one's existing meaning system is; it may be confusing, fragmented, contradictory, superficial or wholesome. If it is wholesome, it just needs maintenance but the other kinds of meanings need change. One can use one's conscience and moral courage to examine the strengths and weaknesses of one's existing meaning, to explore the major meaning systems, and shape a deep meaning system. Inspiration and ideas from great people who have shown deep wisdom and broad love--those who promote openness to knowledge, peace, compassion, and goodness--can be very helpful. I believe the ideas discussed in this book about conscience and human needs can be of great benefit in shaping a good system of meaning.

CONSCIENCE AND MEANING

Utilizing our conscience well and having a deeper meaning system go hand in hand. When we use our consciences well, we are utilizing our capacity to evaluate, reflect, understand, act responsibly, and reassess our actions based on the results. These same activities help to provide deeper meaning. The openness of mind, empathy, responsibility, demand for fairness to all, and respect for truth--all of which are promoted by conscience--get people deeply involved in life. Secular or spiritual (often religious) meanings or philosophies of life that are hateful, violent, unfair, and exploitative oppose the function of conscience.

If one's meaning system contradicts one's conscience, it is a set up for ongoing deeper conflicts or unhealthy defenses to cover up these conflicts. It is interesting to note that St. Paul's insight that faith can be severely damaged by not using conscience (1 Timothy 1:19) is not at all given the importance it deserves. Faith damaged by not using conscience can be seen in numerous cases where religion goes against the spirit of love, compassion, wisdom or goodness. This problem is worst in various religious extremisms. Even moderate religious groups often do not seem to address this problem adequately, if at all. St. Paul's statement in 1 Timothy 1:5 is worth serious consideration: "Now the end of the commandment is charity out of a pure heart, and of a good conscience, and of faith unfeigned."

In our times we are exposed to various cultures, historical and scientific information, religions, and ideologies. If we inform our consciences with such knowledge and consider what is reasonable and fair, we will naturally have a deep meaning system. It goes quite contrary to our consciences and genuine spirituality if we ignore good information easily available and maintain old, narrow, irrational, and unfair meaning and values. Conscience, if properly used, can help us integrate scientific knowledge and spiritual beliefs instead of compartmentalizing them or distorting one, usually science, to fit the other.

I have met many people whose deeper spirituality were stimulated by TV programs and books about NDE, mythology, different religions, and twelve-step programs. Anil was one of them. He had been serious minded, intellectually curious, and good-natured from childhood. His family belonged to a fanatical Christian group. By the time he was eighteen he could not stand his church because of its unfair attitudes towards outsiders, its teachings against science, and its hypocrisy and superficiality. He rejected religion altogether for a few years.

Then television programs on spirituality such as Bill Moyer's interviews of Joseph Campbell revived his spiritual interest. Gradually, he developed a deeper spirituality different from the fanatical religiosity he had rejected. When I asked him about what happened to his peers in his former church, he explained that they went in two different directions. One group became fanatically devoted to the church and put much of its energies into promoting the church's interests; he called them "church pushers." The other group pursued possessions, power, and pleasure including abusing and selling drugs; he called them "drug pushers." Both groups were superficial in their lives. Anil had kept his conscience awake and developed a healthy meaning after rejecting both fanatical faith and no faith.

Deep meanings focus our energies, integrate our resources and give more power and greater fulfillment to our lives. Deep secular and deep spiritual meanings and proper use of conscience go together. Spiritual meaning is obviously an essential part of spiritual fulfillment.

CONCLUSION

"This at any rate is my advice, that we should believe the soul to be immortal, capable of enduring all evil and all good, and always keep our feet on the upward way and pursue justice with wisdom. So we shall be at peace...."[55]

Plato

"The greatest of man's spiritual needs is the need to be delivered from the evil and falsity that are in himself and in his society."[56]

Thomas Merton

For Plato who recommended that we always pursue justice with wisdom, justice meant harmonious functioning of the three elements of the mind--reason, desire, and spirit. Our desires are connected with our needs. Our explorations of human needs and the function of conscience as well as superego show that conscience is our best harmonizing and integrating faculty. This is so because conscience guides one to make good choices to handle one's needs with openness of mind, awareness of choices and their consequences for oneself and others, and one's responsibilities as well as rights. With the guidance of conscience and a good perspective on our needs, we can enjoy material and sensual blessings without being possessed by our possessions or enslaved by our passions, and handle other needs in fulfilling ways. Thus we can foster health, harmony, and happiness individually and collectively.

As we have explored our two inner guides and our various needs, it is clear that promoting the use of conscience and a broad perspective on human needs can be wonderful common grounds for spirituality and mental health.

By and large, conscience has been neglected and misunderstood in the mental health field. Freud contributed greatly to the understanding of human psychology, especially regarding the unconscious, but his idea that conscience is just a part of superego has caused much confusion. While keeping the useful insights of Freud regarding superego, it is extremely beneficial for us to add a good understanding of conscience. As explained in Chapter Two, superego is a very useful inner guide, especially in our social life. When superego conflicts with conscience, the genuinely spiritual or ethical person would follow conscience.

Freud's discovery of psychological defenses which are unconscious has been very useful in psychiatry. But I believe it is even more important for us to be aware of our spiritual defenses (our somewhat conscious manipulations of our consciences) and find better ways to handle our needs. While we are not ethically responsible for our unconscious actions, we are responsible for the conscious choices involved in our spiritual defenses. Reflecting on our pattern of making choices, meditation, and listening to constructive feedback from others are very useful in keeping us aware and alert about our defenses, needs, and healthy options. Psychological and spiritual insights regarding human behavior and motivation can add greatly to our wisdom.

Freud viewed religion as a universal neurosis. I think religions have many healthy aspects (promoting love, wisdom, courage, and caution) and unhealthy aspects (promoting the opposites of the healthy) as I have described in *The Two Faces of Religion*. Healthy religion fosters conscience.

Religious groups can promote conscience or their particular brand of superego which deviates more or less from conscience. Many of the moral codes or traditions of different religious groups are in harmony with conscience, but many others may go against conscience. Among the best things religions do in tune with conscience are promoting love, compassion, and wisdom with all their accompanying features and fruits in the lives of individuals and groups. Among the most destructive things approved or even prompted by religious superegos are closed-mindedness, exclusiveness, superficiality, exploitation, arrogance, meanness, hatred, and violence. The best antidote for such sick religiosity is therapeutic doses of conscience. Many times religious reformers have stimulated people's consciences to move from sick religiosity.

As religious extremism and religiously motivated or supported violence continue to plague the world, there is tremendous need for stimulating people's consciences. As we deal with these extremists, I believe, it is wise for our leaders to go beyond excessive reliance on a paradigm of punishment for wrong deeds and reward for good behavior. It is highly beneficial for our leaders to use their consciences and stimulate consciences of their own followers and the extremists or at least the moderate sympathizers of extremists. It is also crucial to avoid reinforcing unhealthy superegos on either side.

In recent times, there are increasing numbers of people who call themselves "spiritual but not religious." Many religious followers and scholars have concerns that such people are selfish and lack commitment to ethics and good causes. While such concerns have some realistic basis, I have encountered numerous people who are spiritual but not religious who are highly ethical and strongly committed to good causes. Many of them have found organized religions unsatisfactory. For such people insights into conscience and human needs can provide useful guidelines for life.

Since conscience guides us to make good choices, all psychiatric conditions can benefit more or less from utilizing conscience. The role of conscience is less important in severe mental illnesses like Schizophrenia where the cause is mainly biochemical, and the treatment is primarily medication. Even in such conditions, patients who use their consciences are more compliant with treatment, handle stresses better, and relate better to others.

Many other psychiatric conditions can benefit tremendously from using conscience in dealing with various needs. Such are addictions, personality disorders, depression, anxiety disorders and compulsions, sexual dysfunctions, and relationship problems.

As noted in Chapter Two, seven of the twelve steps of AA are related to using conscience well. These steps and learning healthy ways to meet various needs, especially the needs for comfort and pleasure, are important keys to recovering from addiction. Many addicts relapse because they stop using their consciences to guide their choices and take unreasonable risks. Such risks include the argument, "I can safely use this drug or alcohol just this one time" and being in situations that are too tempting to abuse alcohol or drug, in spite of previous experience of relapse under similar situations. Stopping participation in support groups and discontinuing communication with one's sponsor are other unreasonable risks addicts take. Since addiction is also often related to the lack of deeper meaning and satisfaction in life, it is wise for addicts to overcome this deficiency using conscience and an overall view of their needs.

People with personality disorders are among those who can benefit tremendously from the ideas and insights presented in this book. According to psychiatry, personality disorder is a persistent pattern of maladaptive behavior. From a spiritual angle, personality disorder or character defect involves a habit of handling one's needs out of tune with conscience. I have helped numerous such people transform by using the guidance of their consciences in meeting their needs or in delaying or denying satisfaction of certain desires or urges related to their needs. People who are used to immediate gratification of certain needs suffer much tension when they attempt to delay or deny such satisfaction. "Healthy pacifiers" such as relaxation techniques, healthy pleasures, exercise, spiritual practices, and support from family and friends help to defuse the tension. In fact, I have found these approaches to be the most efficient in treating personality disorders.

Strict superego, by causing excessive guilt or shame and making the personality rigid, plays a significant role in many cases of depression, anxiety, and sexual problems. Usually people with very strict superegos have excessive need for being in control, and they tend to hate themselves when they fail to meet their important goals. Such people naturally have problems in their relationships to themselves and others. They tend to use excessive psychological and spiritual defenses, thereby limiting their awareness of their problem. So they have much resistance to change.

Loose superego is often associated with selfishness, superficiality, and problem of irrational gratification (PIG). There seems to be more problems from loose superego rather than strict superego among the younger generation because of their permissive social conditioning. People guided by loose superego also use excessive defenses. In cases where superego is either too strict or too loose, using conscience as the master guide and modifying superego in tune with conscience works well.

Better understanding of our own and others' needs and following our consciences can improve human relationships drastically. If we examine human conflicts at various levels--couples, families, communities, and even nations--we can notice the underlying problem of people trying to deal with their needs without using conscience properly.

When he was a concentration camp prisoner, Viktor Frankl observed sadists as well as kind individuals among both the Nazi guards and the prisoners. Frankl concluded that there are only two races of men--the decent and the indecent. In my experience, decent people live by their consciences and indecent people do not, and there are many who are somewhere in the middle. With a broad perspective on human needs and knowing how superego functions differently from conscience--and how conscience itself can be confused, deadened, evaded or contradicted-- we can understand why people make wrong choices personally and in groups.

As Thomas Merton suggests in the quote at the beginning of the Conclusion, we have a great spiritual need to be free from the evil and falsity in ourselves and in our societies.

British historian Arnold Toynbee had commented that by freeing India from British colonialism, Mahathma Gandhi freed Britain too. Victimizers do not live by their consciences because they persist in making unfair choices, and victims often do not live by their consciences because of their victim mentality and limited choices. Gandhi, guided by conscience, showed cooperative and creative ways of relating to adversaries and antagonists. Gandhi and Martin Luther King, Jr. are among the great leaders who changed many social and political systems which stifled consciences and promoted unjust superegos. Interestingly, these two individuals were spiritual leaders who used religious forces creatively.

In subtle or obvious ways, when religious groups teach their members values and meaning which are inconsistent with conscience, it may be out of genuine ignorance or from unhealthy way of meeting need for power, meaning, identity, esteem or some other need. As I have used the ideas in this book to help people, deeply religious people like ministers who were using unhealthy superegos previously out of ignorance were among the most appreciative of the insights into conscience and human needs.

It is not high intelligence or educational sophistication--although these can be very useful--that basically makes a person decent or indecent, kind or unkind. I have known numerous ordinary people who live by their consciences although they don't use intricate moral reasoning, but rather the goodness of their hearts and the openness of their minds. In complex and confusing situations, they seek the advice of experts.

Superego may give healthy or unhealthy guidance while well-informed conscience gives consistently healthy guidance. In the past, ignorance and social and political restrictions limited people's capacity to live by their consciences. Now, thanks to more knowledge and freedom we can live by well-informed consciences.

Still there are many forces that harm the functioning of conscience. Mistaking superego as conscience and following harmful group values cause major problems. There is strong temptation for addiction, extremism, and gaining sweet success by using manipulative or violent means. Dog-eat-dog competition can take large bites out of conscience. So can fanaticism and legalism. Intense feelings stimulated by internal and external sources sway us away from the guidance of conscience. Superficiality prevents proper input into conscience and misleading propaganda lulls conscience. By using the guidance of well functioning consciences, we are being good to ourselves and truly good to our societies even as we reject unreasonable social trends and pressures.

We can utilize insights into various human needs for our overall well-being. While dealing with our psychological needs, we have to keep our spiritual needs in perspective as well if our lives are to be truly fulfilling. Spirituality emphasizes the deeper meaning of life, wisdom, love, and dealing with our needs using conscience. This is an integrated view of spirituality involving every-day, concrete choices with underlying values and deep meaning. These choices are reflected in our relationships to ourselves, others, and the spiritual realm. Although we cannot expect to be perfect, we can strive to make good choices within our limits.

A life that balances psychological and spiritual needs fulfills those two essential aspects of our being in the world. Listening to conscience and utilizing the great potential at our disposal as we deal with our complex needs, we can fulfill our hearts and souls and help others to do the same. To achieve this, we have to give up superficiality, excessive defenses, and self-defeating selfishness. But it is like caterpillars giving up their cocoons to become butterflies. Let us spread our wings and enjoy fulfilling lives as we strive to reach our full potentials.

Appendix

1. Three Meditation Techniques

The first two of the following meditation techniques use concentration or focusing. As we develop and maintain the skill to focus well, we can use this skill to focus on what is useful, instead of being distracted. The third technique described below, mindfulness meditation, helps to enhance our awareness of what is going on in and around us. All the meditation techniques and the visualization technique I will describe are useful for relaxation.

1) A Sitting Meditation

In a quiet atmosphere, sit safely and comfortably with your back and neck straight (not stiff). Keep your hands comfortably in your lap or on your knees. Let your eyes stay closed and breathe normally. Focus your mind on part of your breathing—either on the movement of air in and out through your nose, or on the back and forth movement of your abdomen, as you breathe. Your mind tends to wander; as it wanders, try to gently bring it back to your focus and let distracting thoughts go. Start practicing for a few minutes and gradually build up to 20 minutes; daily practice of 20 minutes is recommended by many meditation teachers.

2) A Walking Meditation

You can walk back and forth or in a circle. Make the distance long enough to be comfortable for you. If you are walking in a circle, make it large enough so that you don't feel dizzy. Focus on one aspect rather than the whole process of walking; for example, concentrate on the movements of your legs, ankles, and feet.

Choose a very slow but comfortable pace so that you won't have difficulty in keeping balance. Keep your hands stationary, one hand supporting the other at about the level of your navel.

Walk with your head and neck straight and your eyes looking down a few feet in front of you. Let distractions go.

3) Mindfulness Meditation

Start in the sitting meditation position, focusing on breathing; then allow your attention to notice any bodily sensation like pain, tingling, or pressure, or any thoughts or feelings as they come into your awareness. Just notice these without reacting to them. Do this for 20 minutes.

2. The Method of Centering Prayer

The Centering Prayer, a practice based on centuries of Christian contemplative tradition, was popularized in recent times by Catholic monks Thomas Keating, Basil Pennington, and William Meninger. To practice this, choose a sacred word like *Jesus, Mary, Peace, or Love.* Then, sit comfortably with back straight and eyes closed. Silently use the sacred word as a sign of one's consent to experience God's presence and actions inside oneself. When the mind gets distracted by any perceptions, return gently to the sacred word. Do this for a minimum of 20 minutes, then remain silent with eyes closed for couple of minutes before doing other activities.

3. A Visualization Technique

Suppose you deeply enjoy relaxing at a particular beach on a sunny, gently warm, breezy day, watching the waves and listening to the sound of the waves crashing against the sands. Then, you can use your imagination about relaxing at the beach, as a relaxation exercise, in other situations. Imagine as vividly as possible and include as many senses as you can to make the visualization strong. You might include the touch of the breeze, your favorite aroma which you can connect with the beach—perhaps the salty sea smell, the feel of your feet sinking in the sand, the sights of the waves against the sand, and the like. Similarly, you can visualize various outdoor and indoor settings that you find relaxing. Many people find it very useful to reinforce brief positive statements when they are relaxed; say for instance, "I am loving and lovable."

4. PERSONALITY ORGANIZATION AND PSYCHOLOGICAL DEFENSES

According to Freud, our total personality consists of three parts: the id, the ego, and the superego. The id consists of sexual and aggressive instincts and finds pleasure by satisfying these instincts. The id, like a child, just wants to satisfy its urges regardless of the situation. The ego is the coordinating part of the personality which deals with the external reality and the superego. The ego, like a responsible adult, tries to meet instinctual needs in realistic ways. For instance, the ego tries to meet sexual needs in socially appropriate situations rather than when the urge hits. Good ego strength involves impulse control, judgment based on logical thinking, healthy reality contact, the ability to form mutually satisfying relationships, and the ability to integrate different aspects of oneself into a unified whole.

As the ego tries to balance the demands of the id, the superego, and the external world, many conflicts arise among them. The ego uses various defense mechanisms to reduce the discomfort from these conflicts. The psychological defenses have the following functions: 1) They limit feelings to bearable levels and buy time to adjust to changes. 2) They keep in check sudden increases in sexual and aggressive drives, working like an electrical surge regulator. 3) They reduce the stress of major conflicts with one's superego or with important people in one's life. The following are many of the major defenses:

Denial—-invalidating an unwanted fact, e.g., totally denying the reality of a loss.

Projection-- attributing one's own subconscious feelings to others, e.g., Jane cannot accept being angry with her mother. So she thinks that her mother is angry with her.

Regression--going down to a lower level of functioning, e.g., an adolescent under stress acting like a child.

Reaction formation--or going to the opposite extreme, e.g., acting too nice to someone you dislike very much.

Isolation of affect--separating feelings from thought, e.g., remembering very painful experiences but blocking the negative feelings connected with such memory.

Repression--keeping something out of conscious awareness, e.g., many victims of incest repress the experience, but some event in life might bring it out.

Undoing--trying to nullify a thought or action, e.g., the man who walked three times on the hallway without touching any woman's dress to atone for accidentally brushing against a woman's dress. He just had the compulsion to do this ritual, but he was unaware of the underlying reason.

Introjection--unconscious imitation, e.g., a child unconsciously acting like the child's angry father.

ENDNOTES

[1] Albert Einstein, *Ideas and Opinions* (New York: Crown Trade Paperbacks, 1982), p. 36.

[2] Carl Gustav Jung, *The Collected Works of C.G. Jung*, vol. 18, trans. R. F. C. Hull (Princeton: Princeton University Press, 1950), p. 616.

[3] St. Paul, *1 Timothy* 1:19. All quotes from the Bible are from the King James' version.

[4] Sarvepalli Radhakrishnan, *Recovery of Faith* (New York: Harper & Brothers Publishers, 1995), p. 29. Radhakrishnan was a Professor at Oxford University and later President of India.

[5] Victor Hugo, *Les Miserables*, translated by Lee Fabnestock and Norman MacAfee (New York: Signet Classic, 1987), p. 106.

[6] Ibid., p. 110.

[7] Ibid., p. 101.

[8] Leo Tolstoy, *The Kingdom of God Is Within You* (New York: Cassell Publishing Co., 1894), p. 368.

[9] Leo Tolstoy, *The Works of Leo Tolstoy* (New York: Walter J. Black, Lnc., 1925), p. 23.

[10] Leo Tolstoy, quoted by Walter Kaufman in *The Faith of a Heretic* (New York: New American Library, 1959), p. 9.

[11] Quoted By Viktor E. Frankl, *The Unconscious God* (New York: Pocket Books, 1975), p. 52.

[12] Austin Flannery, O. P., *Vatican Council 2 The Conciliar and Post Conciliar Documents* (Collegeville: Liturgical Press, 1984), p. 916.

[13] Paul Tillich, *Morality and Beyond* (New York: Harper& Row, 1966), p. 69.

[14] Sigmund Freud, *New Introductory Lectures on Psychoanalysis* (New York: W.W. Norton & Company Inc., 1965), p. 61.

[15] Friedman, Tucker, et al. "Does Childhood Personality Predict Longevity?" *Journal of Personality and Social Psychology,* Vol. 65.1, 1993:176-185.

[16] Eva Fogelman, *Conscience & Courage: Rescuers of Jews During the*

Holocaust (New York: Anchor Books, Doubleday, 1994), p. 7.

[17] George Eliot, *The Mill on the Floss*, cited in *The Crown Treasury of Relevant Quotations* (New York: Crown Publishers, 1978), p. 11.

[18] Viktor Frankl, *The Unconscious God* (New York: Washington Square Press, 1975), p. 70.

[19] Robert Louis Stevenson, *Dr. Jekyll and Mr. Hyde and Other Stories* (Philadelphia: Running Press 1994), pp. 66-67.

[20] Harry G. Frankfurt, *On Bullshit* (Princeton: Princeton University Press, 2005), p. 61.

[21] Ibid., p. 61.

[22] Victor Hugo, *Les Miserables* (New York: Penguin Books USA, Inc., 1987), p. 93.

[23] Stephen Arterburn and Jack Felton, *Toxic Faith* (Nashville: Thomas Nelson Publishers, 1991), p. 251, 252.

[24] Martin Seligman quoted by David G. Myers, Ph. D., *The Pursuit of Happiness* (New York: William Morrow & Co., 1992), p. 148.

[25] Abraham Maslow, *Toward a Psychology of Being* (New York: D. Van Nostrand company, 1968), p. 200.

[26] Paul Kennedy, *The Rise and Fall of the Great Powers* (New York: Random House, 1987), p. 540.

[27] Bede Griffiths, *Universal Wisdom* (San Francisco: Harper Collins, 1994), p. 41.

[28] Erich Fromm, *Man for Himself* (New York: Fawcett Premier, 1965), p. 58

[29] Linda Tschirhart Sanford and Mary Ellen Donovan, *Women and Self-esteem* (New York: Penguin Books, 1984), p. 13.

[30] Boris Pasternak, *Doctor Zhivago* (New York: Signet Books, 1958), p. 417.

[31] Thomas F. Cash, Barbara A. Winstead and Louis H. Janda, "The Great American Shape-Up," *Psychology Today*, April 1986, pp. 30-37.

[32] David M. Garner, Ph. D., "The 1997 Body Image Survey Results," *Psychology Today*, February 1997, p. 42.

[33] James H. Kennedy, "Sweet-smelling Cows Turn Out More Sociable," *The Birmingham News*, December 17, 1989.

[34] Karen Armstrong, *The Great Transformation* (New Yourk: Alfred A. Knoff, 2006), p. 397.

[35] Erik H. Erikson, *Gandhi's Truth* (New York: W. W. Norton & Company, Inc., 1969), p. 434.

[36] Theodore Isaac Rubin, M.D., *One to One* (New York: The Viking Press, 1983), p. 115.

[37] Redford Williams, M.D., *The Trusting Heart* (New York: Times Books, 1989), p. xiii.

[38] Lao Tzu, *Tao Te Ching* translated by D. C. Lau (New York: Penguin Books, 1963), p. 92.

[39] Lewis Smedes, *Forgive and Forget* (New York: Pocket Books, 1984), p. 168.

[40] Martin E. P. Seligman, Ph. D., *Learned Optimism* (New York: Pocket Books, 1990), pp. 19-23.

[41] Anthony de Mello, *Awareness* (New York: Doubleday, 1992), p. 67.

[42] Robert Ornstien and David Sobel, *Healthy Pleasures* (Reading, Massachusetts: Addison-Wesley Publishing Company, Inc., 1989), p. 7.

[43] A.M. Allchin, *The Merton Seasonal: A Quarterly Review*, (Louisville, KY: The Merton Center), vol. 19 no.1, 1994: p. 20.

[44] Karl Menninger, M. D., *Whatever Happened to Sin* (New York: Bantam Books, 1978), p. 41.

[45] Terry Clifford, *Tibetan Buddhist Medicine and Psychiatry* (York Beach, Maine: Samuel Weiser, Inc., 1984), p.141.

[46] Albert Camus, cited by Irvin Yalom, *Existential Psychotherapy* (New York: Basic Books, 1980), p. 420.

[47] Jean Paul Sartre, cited by Irvin Yalom. Ibid., p. 428.

[48] Joseph Campbell, *The Hero with a Thousand Faces* (New Jersey: Princeton University Press, 1968), p. 384.

[49] Aldous Huxley, *The Perennial Philosophy* (New York: Harper & Row, 1945), p. xii.

[50] Viktor E. Frankl, *The Unheard Cry for Meaning* (New York: Simon and Schuster, 1978), p. 33.

[51] Abraham H. Maslow, *Motivation and Personality* (New York: Harper &

Row, Publishers, 1954.), p. 149-180.

[52] Abraham H. Maslow, *Religions, Values and Peak-Experiences* (New York: Penguin Books, 1976), p. 68.

[53] Gary Groth-Marnat and Roger Summers, "Altered beliefs, attitudes, and behaviors following near-death experiences," *The Journal of Humanistic Psychology* (Summer 1998) 3:110-125.

[54] William James, essays selected by Ralph Barton Perry, *Essays on Faith and Morals* (New York: The New American Library, 1974), p. 212.

[55] Plato, *The Republic* trans. Desmond Lee (New York: Penguin Books USA Inc., 1987), p. 455.

[56] Thomas Merton, *Gandhi on Non-violence* (New York: New Directions Publishing Corporation, 1964), p. 11.

BIBLIOGRAPHY

The following is a list of books I have used for reference besides the ones listed in the end notes.

Alexander, Franz, M.D. and Thomas Morton French, M.D., *Psychoanalytic Therapy* (New York: The Ronald Press Co., 1946).

Benson, Herbert, M.D., *Beyond the Relaxation Response* (New York: Times Books, 1984).

Chopra, Deepak, M.D., How To Know God (New York: Three Rivers Press, 2000)

Dyer, Wayne W., Dr., Your Sacred Self (New York: Harper Collins Publishers, Inc., 1995).

Erikson, Erik H., *Gandhi's Truth* (New York: W.W.Norton &Co. Inc., 1969).

Gottman, John, Ph.D., *Why Marriages Succeed or Fail* (New York: Simon and Schuster, 1994).

Gottman, John, Ph. D., and Nan Silver, *The Seven Principles For Making Marriage Work* (New York: Crown Publishers, Inc., 1999).

Reininger, Gustave, ed., *Centering Prayer in Daily Life and Ministry* (New York: The Continuum Publishing Company, 1998).

Rubin, Theodore I., M.D., *One to One* (New York: The Viking Press, 1983).

Shirer, William L., *Gandhi a Memoir* (New York: Pocket Books, 1979).

Smith, Huston, *The Religions of Man* (New York: Harper and Row, Publishers, 1958).

Wolin, Steven J., M.D., and Sybil, Ph.D., *The Resilient Self* (New York: Villard Books, 1993).

Xavier, N.S., M.D., *The Two Faces of Religion* (Tuscaloosa, AL: Portals Press, 1987).

Printed in the United States
65057LVS00003BA/211-411